It Happened

IT HAPPENED IN

NEW HAMPSHIRE

Stillman Rogers

TWODOT®

GUILFORD, CONNECTICUT
HELENA, MONTANA

AN IMPRINT OF THE GLOBE PEQUOT PRESS

To Barbara, the teacher and best friend who made me into a writer, and to the memory of The Old Man of the Mountain, which inspired my love of my home state.

To buy books in quantity for corporate use or incentives, call **(800) 962–0973, ext. 4551,** or e-mail **premiums@GlobePequot.com.**

A · T W O D O T® · B O O K

Library of Congress Cataloging-in-Publication Data
Rogers, Stillman, 1939–
        It happened in New Hampshire / Stillman Rogers. — 1st ed.
          p.   cm. — (It happened in series)
        Includes bibliographical references (p. [166]—167) and index.
        ISBN 0-7627-2600-8
        1. New Hampshire—History—Anecdotes. I. Title. II. Series.
        F34.6.R64 2004
        974.2—dc22

2004043284

Manufactured in the United States of America
First Edition/Second Printing

Contents

Preface

When I was growing up in New Hampshire, although we spent a lot of time learning about American history, the schools didn't pay much attention to New Hampshire's own part in it.

Dover, where I grew up, had played a significant role in New England's early colonial saga. But the Dover Massacre was barely mentioned; no teacher suggested that we look for the plaque at the Upper Square. There was no class trip to visit the astonishingly well-preserved garrison house that survived those terrible years.

No one ever mentioned that George Washington had visited Portsmouth, only 12 miles away—much less that he had left town with a black eye. And if the Royal Governors Benning and John Wentworth were ever mentioned, the reference certainly didn't include their eyebrow-raising marriages.

I was an adult before I learned that Paul Revere made his first "The Redcoats are coming" ride to warn Portsmouth that British ships were on their way to secure Fort William and Mary, or that the first real battle of the Revolution took place when local men attacked that fort and removed all its arms and munitions before the ship arrived.

As I watched westerns I never knew that the stagecoaches being chased and robbed were from Concord, New Hampshire. Or that they had sailed around Cape Horn to San Francisco aboard clipper ships.

State history is now on the curriculum for fourth graders, and it's a good opportunity to bring historic events and figures closer to home. Class trips have taken my own children to see how people lived in the Fort at Number 4 during the French and Indian Wars, and to Wyman Tavern, where local volunteers gathered for the march to the Battle of Bunker Hill.

It Happened in New Hampshire relates this state's part in these great events of history, beginning with its first settlements at Odiorne Point and Dover. But more than that, it chronicles some events that will never make their way into serious history books. And those stories often give us a clearer picture of what New Hampshire life was really like.

Whether it's how burglars bungled a bank robbery, how poor George Meserve continued to choose the wrong jobs, how Thomas Edison passed the hat for the Salvation Army, how wartime paranoia roiled a town to divisions that split it for a generation, how mill workers felt betrayed by paternalistic owners, or how a small village learned that enemy POWs could be good neighbors, these stories let us glimpse into past eras far better than those of headline events.

Pannaway:
A Colony Is Born
·1622·

Not very much is known about New Hampshire's first citizen, David Thompson. He first enters history as a clerk at the offices of the Council for New England, the body responsible for handing out lands in the new British colonies on the northeast coast of the New World. The council was the creation of Sir Ferdinando Gorges and John Mason, who had talked the Crown into a huge grant of coastal land north of the Massachusetts colony.

As clerk of the council, Thompson knew of the growing interest of adventurers and investors and of the reports brought back to the mother country by Capt. John Smith, among others. Thompson knew there were profits to be made in fishing and he was ambitious. In 1622—with financial partners Abraham Comer, Nicholas Sherill, and Leonard Pomerie—he made an application for a land grant.

On November 15, 1622, the Grand Council granted them 6,000 acres of their choice in the new territories. Before they could claim all 6,000 acres, however, the Thompson grantees had to build a plantation and occupy it for five years. Under the terms of the grant, they would receive transportation to a suitable place and all the supplies they would need until they were put ashore. The investors agreed that all four would split the land when it was deeded.

Their plan was to create a settlement for fishing and furs, both in high demand in Europe at the time. They reconnoitered the coast and found a prominent point of land at the outer southern shore of the deep Piscataqua River, where it entered the sea. Along the west lay a marsh drained by a small creek. Although the shoreline was little more than a solid rock and boulder-strewn beach, the northwest side was protected from the open sea and led directly to the river. That river provided access to the interior and its fur-bearing animals.

Out to sea, approximately 6 miles, were Smith's Isles, named by Captain Smith in 1614. Smith had reported the waters around the islands as teeming with fish and their proximity would be a boon to the fledgling colony.

Thompson chose these lands for his claim. The claim extended about a mile inland from the shore and ran for tens of miles along the coast, from what is now Rye, and then westward along the Piscataqua River through present day Portsmouth and all the way to Fox Point in Newington.

When David Thompson's group of hardy settlers arrived, they saw that the land had other attributes that fitted their purposes well. There was a small hillock that rose gradually, a proper place for fish flakes, also called stages, platforms of saplings on which they would dry fish. Also nearby were flat grounds for growing food. Adjacent marshes would yield salt hay to feed the cattle and livestock. A semiprotected cove would harbor their fishing boats.

Having found a suitable place, they immediately set about establishing their settlement, which they called Pannaway Plantation. The first project was to build the "great house," which didn't necessarily mean it would be a magnificent mansion. In colonial terms it was the settlers' principle residence, serving as both home and fort, if necessary. The entire party occupied the building during the early stages of the settlement.

Thompson's great house was most likely little more than a thatched log building on a stone foundation with two floors.

The first floor would have had a big fireplace for cooking and the rest of the space would have been used as a common work room, where goods and supplies were stored and equipment maintained. The second floor, which may have been little more than a garret, provided sleeping space for everyone. The beds were hammocks or pallets filled with salt-marsh hay; there were few furnishings in the house other than rough tables and crude benches. And, of course, they had to dig a well for fresh water.

Unlike the other New England settlement at "Plimoth Plantation" in Massachusetts, which was formed for religious reasons, Thompson's was a purely commercial venture. He and his partners intended to generate wealth by selling fish and fur pelts, so the next step for the ten new settlers was the clearing of Flake Hill and the building of fish flakes for drying cod.

The solitary woman of the group, the courageous wife of David Thompson, bore the full responsibilities of the household: cooking, mending and washing clothes, and tending fires, the garden, and the myriad other small tasks of a frontier home.

As soon as the great house was completed and the rudiments of daily life had been established, the settlers began fishing offshore and as far out as the Smith's Isles. The fish they sought were cod, huge fish brought in from a fishing ground that had never before been exploited. The catches were large. Once a good haul was on board, the fish were brought back to the plantation and filleted, the remaining parts used as animal feed or fertilizers for the rocky ground.

The big slabs of fish were then salted and set out on the flake platforms for curing under the sun, a process that took weeks. During drying the air all around the settlement reeked with the strong smell of drying fish. When the fish were finally sufficiently dry, they were packed into watertight barrels and shipped off to markets in England and Europe.

Contacts were made with local Indians and trading for fur pelts began. The pelts, too, were cured, packed, and placed on ships bound for British and European markets. Thompson's relationships with the local Indians were good. He is said to have been friendly and fair in his dealings with them, and there is no record of any problems between the Indian and English communities at Pannaway.

Over time this tiny fishing community was in frequent contact with other similar settlements along the coast. In 1626 they received word that the fishing station on Monhegan Island was closing down. The leader of the Plymouth Plantation, William Bradford, traveled north to bid on its fishing equipment. Stopping at Pannaway, Bradford talked to Thompson about the auction and, between them, they decided that it would be foolish to bid against one another. They entered a single bid and split the equipment between the two colonies.

While there is no record to verify it, it is likely that it may have been at this meeting that Bradford enticed Thompson to leave Pannaway and settle in the Massachusetts colony. Business had not been as good as Thompson had hoped, and in 1626 he picked up and moved with his wife to an island in Boston harbor, today called Thompson's Island. He never returned to live at Pannaway, and his land patent expired because he did not occupy it for five years.

Pannaway was idle for four years, when Gorges and Mason transferred it to Capt. Walter Neale. Then, in the 1660s a settler from the Isles of Shoals, John Odiorne, bought the grant. His family retained ownership of the point for centuries, giving the area its present name, Odiorne Point.

During the late nineteenth century, a number of summer homes and farms occupied the land, but in 1942 the United States government established Fort Dearborn on the site. When the government acquired the entire property, it tore down most of the buildings, erecting in their place huge gun emplacements, buried under faux hills. In the process much of the archaeological evidence of Pannaway was lost.

Today, visitors will find Odiorne Point State Park and the Seacoast Science Center, with programs teaching the importance of the intertidal zone. They can also walk the park's many trails, picking out evidence of the many long years of settlement in this historic spot.

Perfidy and Disaster in Dover

· 1689 ·

The small but prosperous settlement of Dover was peaceful as dawn rose on June 27, 1689. There had been trouble with the Indians in the past, but there was no hint of it that morning. Elizabeth Heard left in a small boat with her children to do errands and visit friends downstream on the Cocheco River.

In the darkness of night, they rowed back toward their home, but approaching the falls of the Cocheco, Elizabeth was suddenly brought to full alert. Loud and threatening voices immediately aroused her suspicions. She had witnessed Indian troubles before and had even saved an Indian's life. She knew that some terrible evil was afoot.

Hers was but one of several families living in Dover on small farms only recently cleared from the forest. Their homes were small log buildings of two rooms on the first floor, separated by a massive chimney, and a large loft room on the second floor, which overhung the lower floor. Called garrison houses, they had narrow slits cut in the walls through which firearms could be fired, and they served as both home and tiny forts. As additional defensive measures, five of the garrison houses were surrounded by sharp pointed log stockades. Every family was assigned one of these houses as a place of refuge in case of attack.

Maj. Richard Waldron, a successful shipbuilder and sawmill

and gristmill owner, was the chosen leader in the community, and he took charge of the defenses of the community. His was the most important fortified garrison.

The settlers had reason to protect themselves. Chief Metacom of the Narragansett Indians of Rhode Island, referred to by the colonists as King Philip, had formed a confederation of New England Indian tribes to resist further expansion of English settlements. In 1675 Metacom launched his confederation into a war on the English settlers. King Philip's War spread all over New England and brought terror to the little settlement at Dover.

After the initial series of Indian attacks had subsided, Major Waldron was summoned to a conference in Massachusetts to determine how to prevent further attacks. The colonial leaders developed a plan, which called for a day of athletic contests to which all of the local Indian tribes would be invited. The colonial leaders knew that the Indians liked these contests and they were sure that the chiefs and warriors would attend. Once assembled, King Philip's unsuspecting warriors would be captured and sent to Massachusetts for punishment. Waldron did not think well of the plan but he agreed to hold the contests at Dover.

More than 400 Indians came for the contests, and during one particular event, a gun was fired as a signal for the capture of the Indians. Many of the natives were instantly captured while a few escaped into the brush. One young Indian, terrified by the attack, escaped and hid in the house of Elizabeth Heard. Finding him hiding in her house, she shielded him from capture and death when other settlers came looking for him and he safely escaped.

The captured chiefs were taken off to Massachusetts and enslaved and many were hanged. As many as 200 other Indians were herded onto ships and sent to England as slaves. But some of the enslaved warriors managed to escape and return to their tribes, seething with hatred and planning their revenge.

A chief of the Penacook tribe, Wonalancet, was among those who escaped. A former friend to the English colonists, he was their sworn enemy from that day on. The Penacook and other Abenaki Indians joined together in planning their revenge for the tragedy caused by the deceit of Major Waldron and the Massachusetts authorities.

For twelve years the Indians nursed their hated quietly, while the settlers fell into patterns of carelessness. The sight of Indians in the neighborhood became common over the years, and it was not unusual for them to be allowed to spend nights in settlers' homes. People were negligent about locking doors and stockades fell into disrepair. Waldron himself, when approached about the danger from the Indians, advised the settlers that they should worry about their farms, and he would worry about defenses. He was sure of the friendliness of his docile Indians.

In the spring of 1689, word came to Chelmsford, Massachusetts, from two friendly Penacook Indians that a renewal of attacks was imminent. Quickly, word was sent to Governor Bradford of the Massachusetts Bay Colony, who sent word to the New Hampshire settlers. They should, the governor warned, be on alert for attacks aimed particularly against Major Waldron. Bradford's alert first went to Justice Weare of Hampton, who sent it on by messenger to Waldron's son who lived in Portsmouth.

But the alert was too late. The night before the message arrived, several Indian women begged permission to sleep within the stockades of the Dover garrisons and were allowed to do so. In the middle of the night, the women quietly rose and went to the gates, opening them and allowing warriors into the enclosures. The attackers quickly roused the sleeping settlers, killing the men and seizing the women and older children. Many of the younger children were killed; they would be too much of a problem on the march to Canada.

When Elizabeth Heard landed her boat, she decided to bring her family to the Waldron garrison. Arriving close by, she found the stockade closed and guarded by an armed Indian at the door. Sending her children off to hide, she stayed on. But soon she was discovered by an Indian warrior who came up to her and stood above her. Studying her intently, the warrior looked down at her and then turned away. A short while later he returned, again studying her carefully. Once again the warrior turned, calling out as though he had just killed a settler, and ran away. Her compassionate deed of a dozen years earlier had been repaid.

Meanwhile, Elder Wentworth was guarding widow Heard's own garrison house, which was under attack. As one Indian tried to enter the door, old Elder Wentworth furiously pushed him out and then lay on the floor with his feet against the door, keeping it closed while he screamed for help. Aroused, the others in the garrison house awoke and aided him, eventually driving off the attackers.

Major Waldron was not so lucky. The night before the attack, he entertained Chief Wahowah, and when the chief asked him if he was worried about strange Indians in the area, Waldron dismissed the concern. But now warriors forced their way into the garrison and went to the major's sleeping chamber. Waldron, who was more than eighty years old, grabbed his sword and for a while held off the intruders. Turning to get his pistols, he was felled by a blow to the head and captured. Outside, Elizabeth crept up on the beleaguered garrison and lay hiding in the underbrush.

When all of the household had been captured, Waldron was placed in a chair on top of the table where he had entertained Wahowah the previous night. The captured members of the family were made to prepare food for the captors while they taunted and tortured the major. One by one the warriors came to him, slashing him with their knives as retribution for the massacre of 1676. At last, weakened by the loss of blood, he toppled over on his own sword, which had been propped under him.

From her hiding place, Elizabeth heard the yelling and screaming within the garrison. Finally, the Waldron garrison burst into flames and the warriors departed. It wasn't until the roof crashed down upon the ruins of the garrison that she felt safe to try to find her family.

She was one of the few lucky ones. During the course of the attacks, all but her garrison in this part of the settlement was destroyed. Her children were safe. Twenty-three of the settlers died and twenty-nine others were captured and marched off to Montreal and slavery. Armed parties of men, alerted by the few men who escaped, followed the attackers and recaptured three of the stolen children in the White Mountains, but most of the others either died on the long forced march or were sold into slavery or ransomed.

The Waldron garrison was on the northern slope of a hill that rises from the falls of the Cocheco. Today, the site is in the center of Dover's downtown commercial district, and a plaque at 448 Central Avenue marks the spot of the attack. Visitors can still see what the place looked like by visiting the Dam (also called Dame) Garrison. This log garrison was built in 1675 in the Back River section of the city and survived the attacks of the Indian wars. It was subsequently moved to its present site at the Woodman Institute, 182–192 Central Avenue, where it is in a remarkable state of preservation.

War on the Frontier
·1747·

It was early spring in 1747 when thirty soldiers from Massachusetts anxiously looked out from their log fort. Strange sounds told them that all was not well. They suspected an imminent attack by French and Indian marauders, but had no way of knowing that the force arrayed against them contained more than 700 men.

First settled in 1740, during the French and Indian Wars, the settlement was called Number 4, the fourth in a series of towns established by Massachusetts to protect what it thought was its western border. But in 1741 a more accurate survey made the new settlement a part of New Hampshire. Near the small fort, there was fine fertile land for farming, and it was situated high enough above wide nearby Connecticut River to be safe from flooding. The surrounding forests supplied plenty of pine and hardwoods for its buildings and cooking fires.

It was more than 40 miles to the nearest English town, and the new settlement sat squarely where the Crown Point Trail through Vermont crossed the Connecticut River, both of which were major Indian routes from the north. Soldiers at the fort could give warning to settlements to the east and south of impending French and Indian attack. But it was also a very dangerous place to be.

Times were difficult for the new settlers. The continental aspirations of the French and British kings spread to North America, fanning the flames of war. The French, with their small commercial colony along the Saint Lawrence River, and their Indian allies wanted to stop the expansion of the more vibrant British colonies to the south.

For New Englanders war meant a continual series of raids on outposts spread along the northwestern side of the British colonies. Raiding parties of Indians, often led and accompanied by French officers and soldiers, came down from French Canada over Lake Champlain and the Green Mountains. Others came overland through Crawford Notch and into northeastern settlements.

The Connecticut River Valley, as far south as Deerfield, Massachusetts, was plagued by Indian raids. Men and women working in fields were under constant threat. By 1743 it was obvious to the Number 4 settlers that they must have a fort to protect themselves, but Massachusetts no longer had any interest in spending money on a settlement that was in New Hampshire. Authorities in Portsmouth thought the settlement too far from New Hampshire's other towns and therefore indefensible. So without help, the determined settlers met and voted to fund the project themselves, allotting 300 pounds for it, a large sum of money for the times and for their circumstances. There were barely a dozen families in the settlement.

Their first task was to move most of the houses they had built. They brought thirteen buildings together and arranged them in a large rectangle, connected to one another by sheds and barns. They formed an inner courtyard, while along the outer sides of the buildings, a log palisade 10 feet high was erected, 20 to 40 feet from the inner group of buildings. The palisade logs were set into the ground so that a four-inch space was left between each to allow defenders to fire at attackers.

It was fortunate that these few families worked so hard to complete their fort. While Number 4 suffered few attacks during 1744 and 1745, the following year they had every reason to be thankful for their investment of time, labor, and money. In 1746 the war between Britain and France came to the New World.

French-led raiding parties were sent against many frontier towns. In response, Gov. William Shirley of Massachusetts, without the knowledge of the Crown, put together a New England militia that seized the major French fort, Louisbourg, on Cape Breton Island in Nova Scotia. The French, in turn, redoubled their attacks on the frontiers.

In mid-April 1746, about forty French-led Indians attacked Number 4, burning the sawmill and taking three captives. The raiding party then went south to attack the settlement at Upper Ashuelot (now Keene), burning several buildings and taking more captives. Two weeks later, as the men at Number 4 set out from the stockade to tend to the cattle, they were attacked and one settler was killed. It was now obvious that it was not safe to be outside the gates unguarded.

Even though the settlement at Number 4 was within New Hampshire, in late May Massachusetts sent a company of horse troops to protect it because Gov. Benning Wentworth of New Hampshire declined to help with its defense. After turning their horses out to graze, the newcomers decided to look at the place where the last raid had occurred. It was a bad decision. The poorly armed group was set upon by another party of Indians, suffering a loss of five dead and one captured.

Shortly after, another group of Massachusetts soldiers arrived to reinforce the small fort. They left the fort on July 19 to gather their horses from pasture some distance away. As they approached a low hill, their dogs began to bark vociferously, a sure sign of Indian presence. Lying in wait were 150 French-led Indians. Their ambush discovered, the Indians rose from their hiding places to attack but were driven off, incurring a number of casualties.

August saw even more incursions, with the fort besieged for two days, outlying buildings burned, and cattle and farm animals killed. As fall began, the military season came to an end and Massachusetts decided to withdraw its troops. The people of Number 4, realizing it was not feasible for them to stay the winter without militia, left the fort by December. The fort was deserted except for a dog and cat that were left behind.

In the spring, however, Massachusetts reconsidered its decision about troops and sent Capt. Phineas Stevens and thirty soldiers to defend the fort against new intruders. They arrived on March 27, 1747, and found the fort still sound, undamaged, and inhabited only by the old dog and the cat. Their timing was flawless. While they had been making their way north from Massachusetts, a force of more than 700 French and Indians, under the command of French General Debeline, was marching south through the wilderness of Vermont. Early in April, settlers and soldiers at the fort awoke to dogs barking and acting strangely, and they knew that trouble was at hand. Firing first at a sentry, the invaders then set fire to old fences and grasses around the fort and fired on the defenders.

Cleverly, Stevens prevented the attackers from finding out how few men he had, and even while they were keeping up an effective fire, he had some of his men dig trenches outside and along the walls. The trenches were deep enough for his men to stand up in, protecting them from enemy fire while they were throwing water on the walls to put out fire arrows.

After a short battle, the French general called for a cease fire and sent three men to parley with the defenders. They demanded immediate surrender in exchange for a guarantee of the lives of the defenders. A vote was taken and to a man the defending soldiers refused to surrender, even though they were outnumbered 30 to 700. The fighting immediately resumed, carrying on until noon on the following day.

The French commander again requested a cease fire so that talks could take place. This time his demand was not surrender but an offer of French withdrawal if the defenders would sell them supplies. In his report to Governor Shirley, Captain Stevens related his position: "Selling them provisions for money was contrary to the laws of nations; but if they would send in a captive for every five bushels of corn, I would supply them."

The defenders had had little chance to eat or to sleep. With the refusal of the French bargain, firing began again. Surprisingly, after only a few shots, the firing suddenly stopped. General Debeline, his French soldiers, and Indian allies withdrew and Number 4 was saved. Captain Stevens's little troop had not only beaten a force of 700 but had suffered casualties of only two men slightly injured. And they had secured the valley for future settlement.

Number 4 was located in what is now the small business district of Charlestown. Unused after the end of the French and Indian War, the fort had totally rotted away by the 1760s. A complete and authentic replica has been built a short distance north of town, along the banks of the Connecticut River. Interpreters there portray the life of those first settlers. Each summer reenacters assemble to recreate the battles that took place here when Number 4 was the western frontier of the British colonies in North America.

The Governors' Ladies

· 1767 ·

Gov. Benning Wentworth was a happily married man, but after the death of his wife, he yearned for female companionship. In the end he did find a new wife and happiness, but his shocking choice of a bride dashed the hopes of many eligible Portsmouth women and scandalized the leading citizens of colonial Portsmouth. Only a few years later his nephew, Benning's replacement as governor, shocked the city again when he too made an indelicate marriage that again set tongues wagging all over town.

Benning was the oldest of fourteen children born to John Wentworth, a sea captain, merchant, and governor of New Hampshire from 1717 to 1730. Born in 1696, Benning attended a local school and then attended and graduated from Harvard College before taking up the family business. It was probably during one of his three business trips to England that he made the contacts that set the scene for his own appointment as governor in 1741. In 1743 he furthered his career by purchasing the position of Surveyor of the King's Woods, gaining control of the lumber and mast trade.

Married and with three sons, he remained in his father's three-story mansion until, in the late 1740s, he built himself a fifty-two-room mansion, a few miles from Portsmouth's busy commercial area, in a section known as Little Harbor. He and the family moved into their new home in 1750.

Unfortunately, Benning's wife died and, in rapid succession, his three sons died as well. By 1759 he was alone and without an heir. Soon after, he spotted a young woman named Molly Pitman. Entranced, he asked her to marry him. But, poor man, it was not to be for she was in love with another man, a local mechanic by the name of Richard Shortridge, and she refused.

It isn't prudent to anger the royal governor, especially if he is a demi-king. Richard Shortridge had no idea of what was to befall him. Shortly after he and Molly were married, a press gang appeared at his doorway and, without a chance to protest, young Richard found himself on a British frigate headed out to sea. Benning had his revenge, but even the seven years of Richard's absence didn't lead Molly to give up. When Richard finally escaped and returned home, Molly was there waiting for him. But the governor didn't wait that long.

Over on Court Street another young woman had grown up under circumstances less grand than Benning's. Barefoot and a bit bedraggled, Martha Hilton was sure her life would be a rich one. When she was old enough, she moved into the governor's new mansion, working as a helper in the kitchen and as a maid. Over time Martha and the governor became secretly enamored.

The governor loved to entertain lavishly, and it was not unusual for him to have a large party for dinner at his mansion. One particular evening, he held a grand dinner with many of the best families present, including the Rev. Arthur Brown of Queen's Chapel. After the sumptuous feast, the governor leaned over and whispered to an aide, who then scurried off to the kitchen. Without anyone noticing, young Martha Hilton crept in from the kitchen and stood quietly before the fireplace. Rising, the governor looked at the rector and said in a loud voice, "Mr. Brown, I wish you to marry me." A sudden flutter of gasps flew around the richly paneled room, more than a few ladies there probably wondering if they were about to receive a proposal of marriage.

Flustered, the Reverend Mr. Brown asked, "To whom?" "To this lady," Benning replied and the governor motioned to Martha to step forward. The poor reverend temporized, saying that he had not brought his book with him, to which the governor produced his own Bible. "As the governor of New Hampshire, I command you to marry me," he said. With that Martha Hilton, scullery maid and housekeeper, became Lady Wentworth, the first lady of the province.

After a very few happy years, the governor died, but without children. Lady Martha Wentworth inherited the entire estate of Benning Wentworth, including his huge mansion. But the governorship itself stayed in the family.

Benning Wentworth's nephew, John Wentworth, was bright and highly thought of in his youth. After graduating from Harvard College in 1755, he followed the family business and went to Great Britain with the intent to stay there for an indefinite period of time—and hopefully return with his uncle's job. Before he left, however, he had met a cousin, Miss Frances Deering Wentworth, a resident of Boston. Beautiful and talented, she was attracted to John, and he to her. It was therefore a shock to her when John suddenly left town in 1755.

Within the next five years, she met young Theodore Atkinson Jr., of Portsmouth, also a Harvard graduate, known as a devoted and gentle man. He and Frances were married on May 13, 1762, and took up residence in Theodore's father's Portsmouth mansion. Things went pretty well for the happy couple and, except for the fragile health of the groom, they were happy, but childless.

In 1769 young John Wentworth returned from London bearing the titles of his uncle, Governor of the Colony of New Hampshire and Surveyor of the King's Woods. John was more popular than his uncle had been. Years later, even after the American Revolution, he was remembered as a kind man who would stop on the street and give a few coins to children. The new governor bought a house on Pleasant Street and settled in. Directly across his back yard lay the Court Street house of Theodore Atkinson and his wife, Frances.

History does not record anything that transpired during the next two years, other than visits, strictly honorable, that the governor made to the Atkinson household. But poor Theodore's health continued to decline and on Saturday, October 28, 1769, he died.

The funeral was set for the following Wednesday at Queens Chapel. Frances, dressed in mourning black, spent the interim at her deceased husband's side in the old family home, as friends and neighbors called with their condolences. Among them, undoubtedly, was the governor who, we can only surmise, probably spent quite a bit of time with the widow.

Wednesday dawned a cool, bright day as the funeral procession set off along the streets of Portsmouth. The governor ordered that the guns of Fort William and Mary in Newcastle and the guns on board the man of war *Beaver,* at anchor in the harbor, be fired in honor of the deceased, as the cortege made its sad way to the church. The Rev. Arthur Brown, rector, presided over the services and led the prayers at the family tomb.

For the rest of the week, Frances remained in mourning at home, and on Sunday she appeared at services in her mourning garb. She appeared duly grievous of her loss, but the congregation around her had no idea of what was about to happen.

Frances had called in her seamstress and had given explicit orders, she was to make a wedding gown and it had to be done quickly. In fact she needed it by Saturday, November 11. Invitations went out to all of the most important people, and Portsmouth was caught up in a whirlwind of gossip, upstairs and down.

On Saturday all vessels in the harbor were decked out in

their brightest flags, while church bells pealed their joyous welcome to the happy couple and their wedding guests. The governor appeared wearing white silk breeches with a corded blue waistcoat and white coat; the bride, a stunning gown with voluminous petticoats under her bell-shaped skirt. Her hair was piled high on her head, in the fashion then popular in court circles.

Again, for the second time in just a few years, a befuddled Rev. Arthur Brown stood to perform a gubernatorial wedding, the newlyweds sitting in the royal pew under the big canopy, bearing the royal crest. Amid pomp and ceremony the couple led their wedding procession out of the church, anticipating the festive receptions to follow. Behind them, the Reverend Mr. Brown cleaned up, finally leaving the chapel. Lost deep in thought over this second unusual Wentworth wedding, the poor man tripped and fell on the front steps, breaking his arm.

Travelers today can see Benning Wentworth's historic mansion where he wed Martha Hilton, located at the end of Little Harbor Road off of Route 1-A, on the south side of Portsmouth.

A Loyalist's Reward
· 1771 ·

A ship rested at its dock in Portsmouth Harbor on October 29, 1771, when a club-bearing mob boarded and overpowered the guards. Seizing one hundred barrels of molasses, they carried it off, in Portsmouth's very practical version of the later Boston Tea Party. The molasses was not dumped into the water, but customs collector George Meserve, who had impounded it for non-payment of the hated molasses tax, didn't collect the Crown's money for its import.

Imagine growing up in the eighteenth century, son of a wealthy man and loyal to your king. Then, in spite of your best efforts to improve your position, you are vilified and castigated for your very loyalty and success. Such was the lot of poor George Meserve, who lost all for his king.

The Portsmouth of the mid-eighteenth century was a major port of the British North American colonies. The Piscataqua River flowed 6 miles inland from the Great Island, creating an inland port that was free from the rough waters of the open Atlantic. Ships for the Royal Navy had been built along the banks of the river for over a hundred years, and Portsmouth served as the major port for shipping trees for masts and spars to the home country.

Col. Nathaniel Meserve was among those who had made a fortune as a shipbuilder for the Crown, and he operated the biggest shipyard in town at North Mill Pond. Nathaniel was doing so well that in 1749 he built himself a fine new mansion on Raynes Street, close by his shipyard, to house his family of ten children, including four sons who grew up in privilege, favored by Royal Governor Benning Wentworth and his entourage.

In the late 1750s, however, things started to go poorly for the family. The adventurous colonel answered the call to duty by joining the force collected by the New England colonies to attack the French bastion at Louisbourg, on Cape Breton Island. Smallpox, the scourge of the age, broke out and the colonel died. Soon, one of his daughters died, and her death was quickly followed by three of his sons all between 1758 and 1760. George, as the only remaining son, became not only head of the family but sole heir of his father's and of his brothers' estates.

Over the next four years, George did well, acquiring land by using his position of privilege. He then decided to travel to England and try to convince the Crown to reward him for the services that his father had given to the king as a member of the colonial militia. He succeeded, receiving a grant for thousands of acres in what would one day be Vermont.

By chance, he also learned while he was in England that Parliament was about to pass a stamp tax law that would require that everyone in the colonies buy and affix a special stamp to any and all kinds of documents. Every newspaper, deed, will, public notice, handbill, and myriad other documents would have to have one attached. Knowing that every state would need to have a collector to sell the stamps, he applied to become the stamp tax collector for the Colony of New Hampshire and was thrilled when he was appointed. Pleased with his good fortune, he sailed home happy in his success. Or at least he was happy until he reached Boston.

As he had lingered in London, it seems, he was unaware that the new tax was being greeted in the colonies with outright anger and rejection. People railed against this new tax imposed on them without their consent. George was also unaware that word of his appointment had already reached home. George arrived in Boston on September 6, 1765, and five days later he found out that when word reached the citizens of Portsmouth that he had been named collector of the stamp tax, they had burned him in effigy.

He was shocked. How could anyone burn in effigy a leading citizen and loyal servant of the king? After hearing of his humiliation in the streets of Portsmouth, he announced to all that could hear that he would resign his commission. He then went safely, he thought, back home. But word of the resignation had not reached Portsmouth. Greeted by a large crowd of people who weren't there to wish him well, he resigned again and thought this time he was done with it.

When the special stamp paper reached Portsmouth, George wouldn't touch it, so it was sent to Fort William and Mary for safekeeping. Stamps were required to be affixed to all documents after November 1, but that didn't happen in New Hampshire. No one could buy the new stamps, which were safely in the fort and just weren't available. Then, on January 9, 1766, a ship entered Portsmouth harbor and an important package was delivered forthwith to George Meserve. It was . . . his commission as the stamp tax agent.

Even though Portsmouth was the capital of the royal colony it had a very active group of the Sons of Liberty. The Sons were the leaders in the revolutionary movement and included in their membership not only major figures in the community but many of the less affluent as well. The Sons of Liberty were having nothing to do with the hated Stamp Act.

When they got word of the arrival of the commission, the Sons gathered and marched en masse to the door of George Meserve, somewhat rudely demanding that he turn it over. George didn't resist—he had already resigned—and the Sons impaled the official document on the tip of a sword and marched back to the quay where the commission was thrust into the hands of the ship's captain with instructions to take it back from where it had come.

George, the erstwhile tax collector, still hadn't figured it out. He then applied, and was accepted, as a customs collector, but this time in Boston. He served there from 1767 until 1771, by which time he had grown tired of the commute and wanted to transfer to Portsmouth. The collector there was more than happy to switch places, and in January 1771 George took up his new job in Portsmouth.

But peace was not to accompany him. On October 26, 1771, the brigantine *Resolution* docked in Portsmouth. During an inspection George discovered one hundred barrels of molasses that had not been declared. George, good servant of the king, seized the ship. After all, there was a tax of three pence a barrel and the master of the ship had tried to smuggle it in without paying the duty.

Wrong move, George. The Sons of Liberty got word of it and planned a surprise party. As the ship lay at its dock on October 29, the disguised Sons boarded, overcame the guards, and absconded with the molasses. Gov. John Wentworth, another man who couldn't see the handwriting on the wall, issued a reward for information on the brigands, but none was forthcoming and the molasses was never seen again—at least not by representatives of the Crown.

George continued to try to do his job, but the fractious colonists wouldn't cooperate, so he asked Boston for help from the Royal Navy. They sent up the sloop *Swan,* and in 1774 they finally sent the ship of war *Scarborough.* By this time George didn't dare to keep the customs receipts any longer, so he started giving them to Captain Barkley of the *Scarborough.* He even took to staying on the ship overnight when he felt that prudence required it.

The following year was even worse for George, particularly after the Battle of Lexington and Concord. The rebellious colonists had formed a Committee of Safety, which kept a close eye on George. Governor Wentworth himself became uncomfortable and started spending time on *Scarborough.* When the committee finally instructed George to give up the post of customs collector, he got the message. On November 11, 1775, about two months after the governor sailed away, George Meserve escaped to Boston.

He thought, of course, that the rebellion would be quickly put down and that he would return in triumph to resume his position, this time without trouble. He was wrong again. He spent the next several years first in Boston; then Halifax, Nova Scotia; then New York (where he joined Governor Wentworth as a resident of Flatbush); and finally in England, where he died in Hampstead in 1788, a poor man. Staunchly loyal to his king, he never saw the force of the wind that was blowing across his native land.

Land of the King's Masts

·1772·

Masts, those tall poles rising from the decks of English ships to support the sails that drove Great Britain's navy and merchant fleet, were urgently needed. With England's own forests used up, she looked to her new North American colonies for the masts, spars, and bowsprits she needed.

But these were the best trees, the tallest, broadest, and finest, and the colonists wanted them for their own use. If the trees grew on their own land, what right did the king have to claim them? Almost from the beginning there was conflict as individual colonists schemed to outwit and outmaneuver the Surveyor of the King's Woods. Ultimately, the conflict led to the defeat of the king's men and revolution.

Hundreds of years old and standing in small clumps high above their neighbors, some pines rose more than 250 feet into the air and at their base they could be seven feet or more in diameter. These pines were truly the monarchs of the forests, and the king wanted every last one of them for his navy yards. The early colonists sold mast trees to France and the Netherlands as well as England, but this did not sit well with the king, because they were his likely enemies.

In 1691 the king declared that all pine trees with a diameter of 24 inches or greater belonged to the Crown and imposed a fine of fifty pounds, an astonishing sum for the time, for each such tree cut. This decree applied throughout the whole of New England and New York.

The scheme for enforcing the decree took the form of the Surveyor of the King's Woods, an officer charged with the responsibility of enforcement, with the help of four deputies. It was their job to search through the forest and mark each mast tree with three strikes of an ax, forming the "king's broad arrow." They were also charged with the task of making sure that no one cut these trees and that violators were punished.

The mast trees around Portsmouth were soon all marked and cut, and the search for an additional supply inevitably led inland. The king's surveyors traveled up the Piscataqua, Cocheco, Bellamy, Lamprey, Oyster, and Salmon Falls Rivers from Great and Little Bays in search of the great trees. In each new area they would climb to the tops of tall trees and look out from their vantage points for the tops of the giants standing above all the others.

Once located, the trees would be marked with the broad arrow, and then a road would be laid out to the nearest river. The roads had to be relatively level and straight. Some roads in the state still bear the name Mast Road. Land deeds as early as 1667 show that the mast roads became the arteries for inland settlement.

The first step in harvesting one of these giants was to cut a large number of smaller trees to make a cushion on which to drop the mast tree. Then a pair of axmen carefully felled the prize tree, making sure not to split or damage it as it fell. After the limbs were lopped off, two pairs of wheels, 8 feet in diameter, with each pair linked by an axle, were placed over the log, which was then hoisted to rest suspended between them. Some of the behemoths, especially in winter, were dragged to their destinations on specially made sledges over roads iced for that purpose. Then teams of oxen with as many as twenty to thirty animals, dragged the heavy load to the river bank, where it was slid into the river to be floated to Portsmouth.

But the surveyor and his four deputies had a hard time keeping up with the wily settlers. The settlers wanted the trees for timber and boards in their homes and barns. They wanted them also for the ships that they themselves were building along the banks of the bay and its tributaries. And they wanted to hew and saw them into lumber for shipment to Boston and to markets in England and elsewhere.

When it became unlawful to possess boards 24 inches or greater in width, settlers merely cut the boards to 23 inches and discarded the balance. John Bridger, who held the title of surveyor-general from 1706 to 1720, marked more than 3,030 mast pines during his term but noted that of 70 such pines marked in Exeter, all but 1 had disappeared. One deputy surveyor-general estimated that only 1 of every 500 mast trees made it to England.

In 1736, more than four decades before the battle at Lexington and Concord, the tension between settlers and the surveyor's men led to a violent clash in Fremont, then part of Exeter, known as the Mast Tree Riot. When then Surveyor-Gen. David Dunbar heard about some illegally cut trees in Exeter, he hurried there only to have locals threaten his life. He left, but when he returned with reinforcements, a band of "Indians" attacked and drove them off. It was one of the earliest armed encounters between colonists and representatives of the Crown.

New Hampshire achieved the status of a separate colony in 1741, and Benning Wentworth was named governor. Benning's brother, Mark, happened to be a major exporter of masts and timber to the Royal Navy, so the new governor promptly bought the office and title of the surveyor-general, paying 2,000 pounds for a job that paid only 200 pounds a year.

As governor, Benning had the right to grant townships in the undeveloped parts of his province, raking in some nice profits—and always keeping a good lot for himself. With the office of surveyor of the King's Woods, he also got to reserve the best timber for himself, and of course Mark Wentworth was only too willing to sell it to the Crown. The Wentworth brothers had a lock hold on the mast trade in the Colony of New Hampshire.

These colonists considered it nobody's business which trees they cut. "These frontier people depend on the woods for their livelihood," said Surveyor-Gen. John Bridger. "They say the King has no woods here, hence they will cut what and where they please." And they were deviously ingenious in the ways that they found to evade the mast tree restrictions. They discovered that fire destroyed the usefulness of the trees for use as masts but left them fine for lumber. So they started forest fires, one of which, in 1761, burned 50 square miles in two months.

In 1772 Sheriff Whiting, the royal sheriff, went to arrest Ebenezer Mudgett of Weare, located a bit west of Concord, on orders of Governor and Surveyor of the King's Woods John Wentworth. It seems that Mudgett had been caught in possession of illegal trees. He was arrested and taken before the sheriff, but when he asked for time to come up with bail money, he was released and told to bring in his bail in the morning. Pleased with their day's work, the sheriff and his helper had a good dinner, and probably a bit of hard cider, before they bedded down for the night at a local inn.

Imagine their surprise when, at dawn, a rowdy group of men, their faces painted black, seized poor Sheriff Whiting before he could rise and defend himself. In spite of his valiant struggles, some of the intruders seized him by his arms and legs, holding him while others beat him on his bare back with switches made of small saplings. Angry red welts, as fiery as his own fury, rose on his back.

His deputy, too, awoke to an angry assault and tried to fight off the intruders. Soon, he too suffered a like fate, as switches caused his back to blister. But their ordeal wasn't over. As a final insult, the ears of their horses were cropped, the manes and tails of the animals shaved, and the two were forced to mount their horses and ride back to Portsmouth in disgrace, laughter echoing behind their backs.

The sheriff returned with fire in his eyes and plenty of help and eventually eight of the offenders were caught and hauled before the court. They were found guilty of the offenses, but the sheriff was probably not happy when the penalties assessed against them were fines of a mere twenty shillings each. None received any jail sentence. The price, the prisoners probably felt, was a reasonable one for the revenge they had extracted against the Crown. Even the courts, apparently, disliked the Surveyor of the King's Woods.

The American Revolution was a few years away when Sheriff Whiting tried to punish Ebenezer Mudgett, but the king was thwarted one last time on the very eve of the Revolution when patriots secretly gathered up all of the masts awaiting shipment in Portsmouth Harbor and towed them inland, up the tributary streams, and out of reach of the king's men.

America's First Battle of Independence
·1774·

Four months before Minute Men gathered in Lexington to fire "the shot heard 'round the world," the first battle of the American Revolution had already taken place in New Hampshire. And it was complete with a warning ride by Paul Revere.

People in the Colony of New Hampshire were not very happy with England's King George III by the time 1774 rolled around. The king's customs agents and magistrates routinely searched people's houses at will trying to find smuggled goods, contraband, evidence of nonpayment of taxes, disloyalty, and other possible wrongdoing. Often these searches were made on the basis of mere suspicion, unverified anonymous reports, and unjustified hunches. People were harassed in their homes and at places of work. As elsewhere in New England and the southern colonies, a Committee of Correspondence composed of leading local citizens had been formed to present demands for change. John Wentworth, New Hampshire governor Benning Wentworth's nephew and successor, fully backed the king's excesses and tried to stifle local unrest. He might have done better to listen to it.

As the year 1774 opened, the tenor of the times and the feelings of people on the seacoast were well expressed by the "resolves" of a meeting held in Hampton. They stated that in consideration "of the unreasonable, and unconstitutional power and claim which the Parliament of Great Britain have assumed over the rights and properties of his Majesties loyal subjects in America . . . Upon due and deliberate review of the oppressive measures, which the Parliament of Great Britain have, and still are daily taking to subject the colonies to taxation, and the unjust purposes for which they have exercised that presumed right, it must be evident to every one, that is not lost to virtue, nor devoid of common sense, that if they are submitted to, will be totally destructive of our natural and constitutional rights and liberties, and have a direct tendency to reduce the Americans to a state of actual slavery."

Strong words to address to a king's representative. The Tea Act of 1773, levying new taxes on tea, was the immediate cause of the Hampton Resolves. The discontent that resulted from the act extended to Portsmouth, a major colonial port. During summer and fall 1774, two tea ships entering Portsmouth Harbor were quietly unloaded. When word of the shipment spread, a crowd gathered, menacing the warehouses of the merchant who imported it and breaking windows in his house. To save himself he was forced to export the tea to Halifax, Nova Scotia.

The closing of the port of Boston, as a result of the Boston Tea Party late in 1773, had caused further fury there, especially after it was announced that additional British troops were to be sent into the city. Boston artisans refused to build barracks for the troops, but Gov. John Wentworth convinced Nicholas Austin, of Rochester, to build barracks for British general Thomas Gage's forces. When the local Committee of Correspondence found out in November, they summoned Austin to meet with them to explain his involvement. When he appeared before the committee, he was made to fall to his knees, confess his role, express sorrow, beg forgiveness, and promise never again to assist British troops.

At that time local militias of the provinces, in the name of the king, maintained the forts of their own provinces, manned them as needed, repaired them, and were responsible for supplying them with canon, shot, powder, and arms. New Hampshire's major fort was the Castle of William and Mary at New Castle, a small island controlling the entrance to Portsmouth Harbor.

It was a run-down affair, its walls and equipment in disrepair, manned by only five soldiers and their commander, Capt. John Cochran. The captain was paid only three pounds a month and his soldiers a mere twenty-five shillings a month.

In September, General Gage raided Charlestown and Cambridge, Massachusetts, and seized arms and munitions of the local militias. Matters became even more critical when the colonies got word in December that the king had ordered that no powder or munitions were to be exported to the colonies.

On December 12, 1774, the Committee of Correspondence in Boston heard that General Gage was about to take further military action. They sent local silversmith and patriot Paul Revere to Portsmouth, and arriving on December 13, he sought out merchant Samuel Cutts, a member of the Committee of Correspondence. Revere told him that "orders had been sent to the Governors of their provinces to deliver up their several fortifications and Castles to General Gage" and that British troops had been embarked on transports to take control of the forts.

Cutts immediately called the local Committee of Correspondence together to discuss the threat. Early the next morning, committee members sent riders to the outlying towns and marched through the streets of Portsmouth, blowing fifes and banging drums to spread the alarm. Two hundred angry men gathered and marched on the fort. As they marched down the street and out past the harbor toward the fort on that cold and snowy day, their numbers grew. Men from New Castle and Rye joined in, until they numbered more than 400 when they gathered at Fort William and Mary at about three o'clock in the afternoon.

Governor Wentworth had warned Captain Cochran to be on his guard, but Cochran was shocked to see this huge number of men surrounding his fort and demanding entrance. He had only five men and himself to defend it, and two of those men had joined him within the previous twenty-four hours. Cochran dared the besiegers to try to enter at their own peril. A howl of derision arose as the crowd yelled back that he should open the gates.

Immediately, Captain Cochran ordered the three four-pounder cannons fired and his men to fire their muskets. With a cry the crowd surged forward on all sides, quickly overwhelming the tiny garrison before they could reload their weapons. The crowd uttered three loud "huzzas" as the king's flag was pulled down. Miraculously, there were no serious injuries on either side. The captain and his hapless men were seized and held prisoner. Demands for the keys to the powder magazine were defiantly refused by Cochran, loyal to his king and governor.

Exasperated, the invaders took axes to the doors of the magazine. Inside they found one hundred barrels of gunpowder, which they immediately began to move out to the fort's wharf on the waterfront. In their searches they also found 3,200 flints, five kegs of bullets, and other military supplies, which were seized and carried off as well. For an hour and a half, as the munitions were taken away and loaded onto gundalows, local sailing barges, Cochran and his men remained prisoners.

Once released, Captain Cochran immediately wrote to Governor Wentworth telling him of the assault and of the valiant attempt that he and his men made to ward off the invaders. The next morning, the streets of Portsmouth rang again to the sounds of fife and drum after the governor ordered Major General Atkinson to go out and enlist—or impress—thirty men into service for the protection of the fort. But alas, by noon the officers in charge of that detail had to report that they could not find a single man to take up arms for the king.

That failure was critical, for while the king's men were out looking for recruits, more colonists from the outlying towns were gathering together to return and seize more of the arsenal of the fort. Under the leadership of Loyalist-turned-dissident John Sullivan, thirty to forty men loaded onto gundalows and in the evening again seized the fort from the unfortunate Captain Cochran.

There is no record of any fight when John Sullivan and his men arrived that night. Again taking control of the fort, they took what powder was left, sixty muskets, fifteen four-pounder cannon, one nine-pounder cannon, a large quantity of cannon shot, and whatever other miscellaneous miliary equipment they found. They had to leave the larger cannon behind because they were too heavy to move. After the second attack, the slow-moving gundalows made the tedious journey back up the Piscataqua River to Great Bay, then up the much smaller Oyster River to Durham. Arriving in Great Bay they found that the river was frozen and so spent the next several days chopping ice in order to get the boats from both excursions to safety.

Quickly and quietly, the powder and stores were parceled out to patriots in towns throughout the region. Durham housed twenty-five barrels, some of which were rumored to have been kept under the church pulpit. Exeter hid twenty-nine barrels, Kingston twelve, Epping and Nottingham eight each, and other smaller towns fewer barrels. Four barrels even remained hidden away in Portsmouth.

On December 17, Governor Wentworth's entreaties to General Gage were finally answered, a classic case of locking the barn door too late. On that date His Majesty's frigate *Scarborough* and sloop *Canceaux* arrived with between eighty and one hundred regular British troops on board. They quickly took over Fort William and Mary.

By June 1775, after the Battle of Lexington and Concord, Governor Wentworth realized that his position in the colony was extremely perilous. With the faithful *Scarborough* hanging offshore, he moved first to Fort William and Mary, then to the Isles of Shoals. On September 21, 1775, he issued his last proclamation before boarding *Scarborough* and heading off to Boston. From that date New Hampshire was free and independent, no longer subject to the king of Great Britain. In 1788 New Hampshire became the ninth state to join the Union.

In 1791 the State of New Hampshire turned the fort over to the new federal government, which changed its name to the more appropriate Fort Constitution. The United States operated it as a fort until 1960, when it was returned to the state. It is now a museum, still sitting on Great Island in the town of New Castle, a monument to the people who refused to let the king take their property and liberties.

War Comes to the Frontier

·1775·

Abner Sanger, who lived in Keene, had long kept a diary of the events in his life. Mostly it recorded the daily events of his life: who he had worked for, the status of crops, and his thoughts on events of the day. But as 1774 came to a close, he wrote of the strain between colonists and the British government. In October he recorded that a neighbor, Benjamin Carpenter, came to his home with the news that two regular British soldiers "go along up and tell at Carpenter's how that Governor Gage is gone round to fetch French and Indians to fight" against the rebellious colonists.

The people were terrified. Here was word that the governor of Massachusetts and head of British forces was trying to again unleash the scourge of Indian attack upon them. The next day, the artillery militia trained in Keene.

While Gov. Thomas Gage had not actually started to organize such attacks, he did, in fact, write to the British Indian Superintendent to find out if the Indians would be willing to wage war against the colonists if the government needed their services. He also subsequently urged the superintendent to remind the Indians that they should only do harm against the king's enemies, and not royal troops.

The people on the western edges of New England had been subject to invasion by native Indians for decades, particularly during the wars between the French and the British, known as the French and Indian Wars. During the King George's War of 1744–48, the newly founded community of Upper Ashuelot (renamed Keene in 1753) was attacked and burned by Indians operating under the aegis of the French in Canada. Many homes and the town meetinghouse were burned and people were killed or taken prisoner to be sold into slavery in Canada or ransomed back to their families.

The Fort at Number 4 (now Charlestown) was heavily attacked during the same period. Again in the French and Indian War, 1755–63, the threat of Indian attack became real. New Englanders united in defense, some 3,400 of them helping in the capture of Montreal in September 1760. Eight hundred of those troops were from New Hampshire. With the threat of Indian attack seemingly ended, the settlement of the borders resumed, with Keene being organized as a town in 1753.

The settlement at Keene was small in 1774, its population only 756 people. It was isolated from the rest of the colony by deep woods. The main roadway, fit only for oxen and wagons, ran north–south through Deerfield and Northfield, Massachusetts. To the east a road extended a short distance before turning into a trail through the woods that was barely passable for a person on horseback. The nearest road to the towns of the New Hampshire seacoast were at New Ipswich, about 25 miles east over rough trails.

But in April 1775 the world changed for the people of Keene and those throughout the colonies.

April 20 dawned clear, cold and frosty, one of those beautiful early spring days that contain the promise of warm sunny days to come. Abner Sanger got up early and went to the home of a friend, David Nims, to square accounts with him. Abner was interested in learning the art of land surveying, so he then went off to the home of Breed Batchelder to borrow the manuscript that Breed was writing on the subject.

Two days earlier in Boston, and still unknown to the people of Keene, Governor and General Gage had told his officers to prepare the troops for an excursion into the countryside to seize arms and munitions that were rumored to be hidden in nearby Lexington and Concord. On April 18, British officers were patroling the roads looking for colonial spies and rebels. That night, troops began to move across Boston Harbor to Lechmere Point in Cambridge. Paul Revere was again chosen to spread the alarm of the coming of British troops, and five minutes after he launched his boat into the Charles River, the order was given that no one was to be allowed to leave Boston.

Before the sun had even risen on April 19, the British had reached Lexington and blood had been spilled. The British moved off toward Concord, while colonial horsemen set off in every direction to spread the word that the king's army had attacked colonial patriots. By early morning of the same day, the word reached Hollis, 42 miles away, and by afternoon ninety-four men set off for the fray. By afternoon word reached as far as New Ipswich, and then to Rindge, 65 miles from Lexington. That same day fifty-four men set out from there.

The rider was tired from his long horseback ride and from Rindge to Keene the trail was rough. It was a perilous ride through the woods at night on a trail that was little more than a path. By mid-morning on April 20 he reached the village of Keene and immediately went to the commander of the Keene militia, Capt. Ephraim Dorman. Captain Dorman was an old and respected member of the community, but he knew that he wasn't up to the task. Together with the rider, he went to Capt. Isaac Wyman, and immediately the three spread word of the attack about town. Abner Sanger confided to his diary that "Keene town is in an uproar."

Keene, then as now, was an attractive town. The wide principal street was lined with large homes, set well back from the dirt road that ran through its center. At the north end of the street stood the town meetinghouse and courthouse, and before it stretched the common, which served double duty as the militia training ground.

No sooner had the rider met with Captains Dorman and Wyman than men and women, boys and girls, were scurrying off to spread word of the British assault upon their own citizens and calling all men to assemble at the militia grounds.

In the gloom of an afternoon rainstorm, they gathered to learn of the killing of forty-nine of their fellow colonists. A vote of the men assembled called for raising a company of militia to "oppose the regulars." Captain Wyman, then fifty-one years old, stood before the people of his town and called for volunteers. Twenty-nine men came forward; Captain Wyman made it thirty. Issac Wyman was chosen captain of the company, Thomas Baker its sergeant, and Jeremiah Stiles its orderly sergeant.

Go home, Wyman told them, and prepare yourself with guns, ammunition, clothing and food for "all the roads will be full of men and you can procure nothing on the way." They were to meet the following day at his tavern on the main street. That night, as the sun set, thirty families in Keene underwent the anguish of preparing to send their husbands, fathers, and brothers off to war.

From the fine houses in town to the lowly cabins on the outskirts, the necessities of life were gathered together, weapons cleaned and prepared, lead melted and poured into shot, and food and clothing carefully packed. Abner Sanger enlisted, but then remembered that he had sold his gun after the end of the French and Indian Wars. He was wondering what to do, when Isaac Estey came to him, offering his own gun to Abner "to fight Regulars."

At dawn on the morning of April 21, thirty men gathered at Captain Wyman's tavern. Because it was cold and a spring snowstorm was in progress, they most likely assembled first in the southeast corner tavern room of the first floor before forming ranks in the front yard. Thirty men, farmers and craftsmen and settlers of the frontier, gathered together to take up arms against the army of their own king. Amidst tears and huzzahs, at nine o'clock in the morning, they marched forward behind their fifer, Samuel Bassett.

On the first day they walked 23 miles through terrible weather, stopping at taverns along the way. Everywhere they went, they found men headed toward Concord. Arriving on April 24, after a hard and wearying march, they discovered that the Battle of Lexington and Concord was over, but that American troops were gathering on the town common of Cambridge.

Having enlisted only for the one battle, most of the men reenlisted at Cambridge for a longer term. Many of the "Keene 30" served with distinction at the Battle of Bunker Hill. Abner Sanger, however, was not among them. After a few days in Cambridge, he decided he wanted nothing to do with the army, returned to Keene, and sat out the war.

A Presidential Black Eye

· 1789 ·

When George Washington was inaugurated as the first president of the United States in 1789, the American people were, for the most part, wary of having a monarch of their own. But many also wanted their chief executive to be shown the respect that the office deserved, and they cast about for a suitable term of address. It is said that Washington himself settled the issue by requesting that he be referred to simply as "Mr. President." Others, however, were very sensitive to any obeisance paid to him and mutterings began to circulate of his monarchical behavior.

Hoping to lay these rumors to rest, the new president began a tour of the states so the people could see and meet him. The trip also served to introduce him to parts of the country that he had not seen and to unify the fractious states. Leaving the capital in New York City, he made his way northward through Connecticut and Rhode Island and arrived in Boston in October. After a grand fete, he left on October 29, 1789, for Portsmouth.

The party left in pomp, with Washington riding a coach and others of the party on horseback. Among them was the president's young personal secretary, twenty-nine-year-old Tobias Lear, who had been recommended to him by Maj. Gen. Benjamin Lincoln. Tobias, who graduated from Harvard

College in 1783, was the son of a well-to-do Portsmouth landowner and shipmaster, and the family still lived in the ancestral home on Hunking Street. Washington became very fond of Tobias and treated him almost as a son. It was a good match with the president: Tobias was to serve as his secretary for sixteen years, until the president died.

Crossing the Amesbury River by ferry, the party moved on, greeted by admirers along the way, until they came to the New Hampshire border on Saturday, October 31. Waiting to greet them were Gov. John Sullivan, himself a hero of the revolution, and John Langdon, a noted New Hampshire patriot. Langdon had recently been selected as the very first Speaker Pro Tempore of the new United States Senate, and had administered the oath of office to the president on June 30 of the same year.

With them were a troop of cavalry and a party of approximately 700 citizens, who had arrived on horseback, by carriage, and on foot. Banners and flags fluttered in the wind and a crowd of onlookers looked hard for their first glance at the hero, their president. In triumph they entered the capital city of Portsmouth, where a wildly enthusiastic crowd awaited. Flags and banner flew and cheers filled the air as the impressive party passed through the narrow streets.

The Portsmouth of those days was one of the largest ports of the new nation. More than 16,000 tons of shipping were to enter the harbor during the coming year. The *Raleigh* and the *Ranger*, the first and second ships of the new navy had been built on Portsmouth ways. Portsmouth was a city at its maritime peak, and it turned out for the president in style.

The roar of thirteen cannons rang out and all the church bells in town pealed their greeting. All the ships in the harbor were rigged in banners and colors, and military bands lustily played martial and popular songs. Mounting to the second floor of the statehouse, Washington was met with a roar of approval when he addressed the crowd from the balcony. So enthusiastic was the reception, in fact, that few heard what he had to say.

In homage to their hero, a new song was written, set to the tune later known as "America," and the crowd joyfully sang:

Long may thy Trumpet, Fame,
Let echo waft the Name
O'er all the world around
Far as earth's utmost bound,
Thy equal is not found,
Columbia's son.

Washington and his visit were clearly very popular and the pageantry and enthusiastic reception seem to have laid to rest any worries, at least here, about his regal tendencies. After the official greeting, the tired president and his retinue walked the short distance to the Brewster Tavern at the corner of Pleasant and Court Streets, where rest and refreshment were provided.

Sunday, as might be expected, was a day for church services, and the president attended a special service at Queen's Chapel, renamed St. John's Church two years later. Its denomination was Church of England and it had been the church of the royal governor. On the center of the north side was a raised pew over which hung a huge canopy carved with the royal arms. Inside, red plush draperies were hung in festoons behind a pair of carved chairs that had been presented by Queen Caroline. Not long before Gov. John Wentworth had occupied the pew.

No one seemed to mind when the president, accompanied by Governor Sullivan, Senator Langdon, and Theodore Atkinson, the state's secretary of state, entered and took his place in the former royal pew. The widow Atkinson had married John Wentworth, the last royal governor, and had fled with him at the outbreak of the war. Following the service, after a brief respite for lunch, the balance of the president's day was spent in the Old North Church. The Rev. Joseph Buckminster—who greeted his distinguished guest with the words, "We hail welcome the savior of his country"—gave a prolonged oration.

Monday was another day of public celebration. The president was brought to the docks where he boarded a red, white, and blue ceremonial barge manned by sailors in white uniforms. Other guests boarded a second barge, this crewed by blue-clad sailors. Behind the official barges another came bearing the town band doing their best to play well in the swells of water. Down the harbor they rowed to its mouth, Washington viewing the city's docks, shipyards and shipping, Fort William and Mary, and the lighthouse at the entrance.

Although the tide was not good for fishing, General Sullivan suggested they give it a try and had arranged for Colonels Cogswell and Hackett to bring tackle and fresh clams for bait. John Langdon put his line in first, while the president baited his own hook and then tossed it in. Langdon caught the first fish and just then Washington's line caught on a rock, jerking the boat and jostling everyone on board.

Suddenly, the strength of the tide freed the hook and the barge leapt forward, upsetting Washington, who bumped into Langdon and then promptly landed, seated on a bait can. Smiling, probably with embarrassment, Washington picked himself up and, rebaiting his hook, tried again, this time hauling in a pollack and a few minutes later a half-pound cod.

But the sea where they fished was rough, and while the official party cast for fish, the poor band languished. Colonel Cogswell writing to his wife later said, "Every one of the musicians was puking sick from the time we left the ledge for Kittery till we landed." Tiring, the party set off for Kittery, where Washington wanted to see an old friend.

As he stepped off the boat, Cogswell noted that Washington continually raised his handkerchief to his eye. In the course of his tumble onto the bail can, the president had struck the corner of John Langdon's tricorner hat and now he had a shiner.

It's a tribute to the awe with which he was held that none of the official nor newspaper accounts of the festivities that followed the fishing trip mention Washington's black eye. The following day, Tuesday, Senator Langdon honored the president with a reception for highly placed friends at his new mansion, and in the evening a banquet was hosted by General Sullivan. Wednesday was dedicated to a visit with Tobias Lear's family, Washington particularly wanted to meet Lear's mother, even with his blackened eye.

When George Washington left Portsmouth for Boston on November 4, he had accomplished his goal. The people of Portsmouth had identified themselves with the presidency and with him as a man. His forthright and friendly manner had endeared him to the populace and fears of a monarchical leaning were banished. Perhaps his very noticeable black eye played a part.

Today, visitors can see many of the places Washington visited in Portsmouth: The Langdon House at 143 Pleasant Street; the Tobias Lear House, on the grounds of the Wentworth-Gardner House at Gardner and Mechanic Streets; and Saint John's Church at Chapel and Bow Streets. The original church burned in 1806, but Washington's chair and the silver items used in the service are on display.

Tragedy in the Mountains

· 1826 ·

The steep mountainsides of Crawford Notch rise starkly on either side, constantly narrowing as the land rises to the passage at the top. Here and there on the slopes are the ragged rocky wounds of landslides, reminders of the terrible slide that took the lives of the Samuel Willey family on August 28, 1826.

As New Hampshire grew in the eighteenth century, people seeking new farmlands moved from the seashore westward and northward into the forests. At the same time settlers from Connecticut and Massachusetts moved northward, following the banks and broad river meadows of the Connecticut River. Between these two streams of migration lay the White Mountains, effectively blocking the movement of people and goods from the new farms of the west and the cities and supplies of the seacoast ports of Portsmouth and Portland.

It wasn't until 1771, on the eve of the Revolution, that Timothy Nash and a hunting companion, while chasing a moose, climbed a tree on Cherry Mountain and spotted a gap in the looming mountains. Nash investigated and then rushed to Portsmouth the tell Gov. John Wentworth of his discovery. The news was important to Wentworth for several reasons. One of his main sources of income was the sale of land grants for new townships; a passage through the mountains would make sales easier by facilitating the shipment of farm goods to market from the new northern Connecticut River townships.

Wentworth and Nash struck a bargain. If Nash could bring a horse from the village of Lancaster through the notch to Portsmouth, Wentworth would give Nash a grant of a huge tract of land in the valley at the head of the notch.

Returning home, Nash got in touch with his friend Benjamin Sawyer and together they managed to ride, drag, and hoist the beast through the narrow opening and get him down over the rocky cliffs and on to Portsmouth. In accordance with their deal, Nash and Sawyer got the grant of land and a road through the notch was started in 1774. The road was steep and rough and it was replaced after 1803 by another.

With the coming of the road, people began to move into the notch, including the remarkable Crawford family. Impressed by the awesome beauty of the wild mountains, they settled and opened their home to visitors wanting to see the mountains and climb Mount Washington. Abel Crawford was a leader who, together with other members of his family, marked the first trail to the summit of Mount Washington. Tales of the wonders of the mountains quickly spread to the cities on the coast, and the Crawfords promoted travel to the area. Others also opened guest houses to accommodate the travelers.

Among these was the family of Samuel Willey, who came to settle in the valley in 1825. At a spot where the Saco River opens into a small level area, they settled into an old house that had stood on the spot for many years and that Crawford had used the previous year to house travelers. The steep slopes of the mountain rose directly behind it and a pasture lay in the valley just below. The house was one and a half stories, with a stable and barn to the side. The family set up housekeeping, started their farm, and opened their doors to travelers in need of lodging and meals.

The Willeys worked hard on the house through the fall of 1825, repairing it where needed, fixing the barn and enlarging it, and getting their gardening done. Through the fall and winter, they found that they had a fair number of guests and looked forward to a good summer in 1826. In June, however, something happened that shook their confidence in their new home. While sitting at a window in the house, they heard a noise and looked up to see a huge landslide start on a nearby mountain and crash into the valley. A short while later, another slide came down the mountain. The Willeys decided that it might be wise if they thought about moving.

Samuel spoke to Abel Crawford about his worries and his intent to move while the two were working together to repair the road that had been damaged by the slide. Crawford pooh-poohed the danger and Sam Willey changed his mind, deciding to stay on. But he did look for a place where he and his family could seek safety should a slide threaten.

The weather that summer was pleasant, but hot and dry. Little rain fell and the ground on the steep mountain sides dried out to an unusual depth, turning to powder and weakening the root structure of the trees and bushes that clung to the steep slopes. It wasn't until late August that a little rain finally started to fall.

On Monday August 28, there was a light drizzle, but the sky darkened in the evening and as night fell it began to pour. It was one of the most fierce storms anyone had seen in the valley. Benjamin Willey, Samuel's brother in Conway beyond the end of the valley, had to help rescue cattle and sheep from flooding meadows. Ethan Allen Crawford said of the storm that "it seemed as though the windows of heaven were opened and the rain came down almost in streams."

In his 1856 book *Incidents in White Mountain History*, Benjamin Willey wrote:

> Lightning and storm, with flash and gusty roar
> Loosened, and on its fearful errand sped
> The rocky avalanche, crashing, strong and blind,
> While Terror stalked before, and Death was close behind.

The next day, settlers downstream were alarmed by the torrents of water, rocks, and debris coming down the rapidly rising river. They rushed about to move their cattle to safe ground. In the late afternoon a visitor named Barker left Ethan Allen Crawford's house and started down the valley. He got as far as the Willey's farm and decided to stop. He saw that there had been a slide but saw that the house was fine. The doors were open, and he was puzzled by the plates on the table, the open Bible, and signs of a sudden departure. The Willey's had obviously left in a hurry. Thinking that they had left to spend the night with Abel Crawford farther down the valley, he curled up in a bed and lay awake worrying about a moaning sound that he heard outside.

In the morning Barker found an ox partially trapped by the damaged barn, the source of the moaning. Now alarmed, he took off down the valley reaching a tavern in Bartlett, where he told of the devastation in the valley. The same night, a party of men set off to the site of the slide, a mass of sand, huge rocks, and broken trees lying in confusion on the valley floor.

Carefully searching, the party of neighbors found no sign of the missing family until about noon on Thursday when the body of the farmhand, David Allen, was found. Soon afterward, Mrs. Willey's crushed and broken body was located and then that of Samuel Willey, all terribly mangled. Two days later, the bodies of another farmhand and the remains of the Willey's oldest daughter were located. The three younger Willey children were never found. The entire farm family of eight persons had been lost in the slide.

The tragic end of the Willey family was the result of an ironic turn of fate. A short way behind the Willey house lay a huge granite outcrop, a big piece of rock left behind by a glacier. As the tumult of rocks, earth, and trees tore down the mountain toward the Willey house, it ran into the rock, dividing into two streams. Passing around the house and knocking the barn down on the horses and cattle, the two streams united again in front of the house, sweeping the helpless family with it. Had they stayed by their hearth, they would have survived.

Word of the disaster spread fast and far. Although the Crawfords had done much to draw the public's attention to the mountains, the tragedy did more. Accounts of the slide and its aftermath filled newspapers around the nation. Soon visitors from the entire New England seaboard were traveling to the site of the Willey home, looking at the rumpled beds, and staring at the Willey family Bible. Nathaniel Hawthorne, after viewing the site that summer, wrote of the hapless Willey family in his *Twice Told Tales*, in the story "The Ambitious Guest."

The deaths of the Willeys and their farmhands brought the mountains to the attention of the American public and, ironically, served as the real beginning of the history of the White Mountains as a tourist destination. Still fascinated by their story today, travelers stop at the site. The Willey house itself burned in 1898, but a cabin at the state-operated rest area has mementos of the Willeys, the slide, and the history of the valley. And somewhere under the surrounding land lie the remains of the three little Willey children. Their parents, once buried nearby, were reinterred in Intervale behind what is now the Scottish Lion, a local shop.

At War with
Indian Stream
·1835·

Indian Stream, at the time of the American Revolution, was a vast unsettled land along the narrow northern tip of New Hampshire. This area, north of the forty-fifth parallel, is along the border with Canada, which was then a colony of Great Britain. But when the Treaty of Paris ended the war in September 1783, the boundary it established left ownership of this huge piece of unsettled land undetermined. It took sixty years of confusion and conflict to settle the issue.

In spite of the uncertainty of title, it wasn't long after the war that frontiersmen and settlers trekked into the Indian Stream territory looking for new opportunities for fur trapping, lumber, and farming. After the hunters and trappers, it was land speculators who headed northward into the territory. The first group of speculators was led by Thomas Eames, who bought land in Indian Stream from an Indian named King Philip. Called the Proprietors of Philip's Grant, the Eames group eventually became known as the Eastman Company. Their deed was quickly recorded in Coos County.

Three men, led by Moodey Bedel, composed a second group of speculators. Their title to the land, not immediately recorded, was signed over to them by a group of Saint Francis Indians who claimed to represent the tribe. They maintained that King Philip's title was not valid. This group called itself the Bedel Company.

Both companies ignored federal law, which forbade individuals to buy Indian lands. Both also ignored the fact that there were now two different companies claiming title to Indian Stream, a sure source of future conflicts over titles to any land grants in the area.

But there were other problems with the titles of both companies. Festering quietly in the background was the other great unknown: New Hampshire claimed ownership of the land, and therefore control of settlement, under the Treaty of Paris. Canada, on the other hand, claimed ownership north of the forty-fifth parallel and east to the Connecticut River because of the ambiguity of the treaty. Therefore, there were four entities that claimed control over the right to sell the land and control settlement.

Except for a boundary survey in 1799, the Eastman Company quietly sat on its hands and did little to encourage settlement. None of the Eastman Company proprietors moved into the territory. The Bedel Company, however, was not idle. Moody Bedel, Nathaniel Wales, and David Gibbs not only moved onto the land and established farms, but they actively sought out other settlers to whom they could sell the land. Thus, the rather disorganized Bedel Company occupied the land, while the highly organized Eastman Company only talked about it. New Hampshire and Canada did nothing to assert their claims in the beginning.

Under the leadership of the Moody Bedel group, gristmills and sawmills sprang up along the streams and more settlers put down roots in spite of the War of 1812. The Treaty of Ghent, between England and the United States, which brought the War of 1812 to an end, still did nothing to settle the boundary issue.

Starting in 1819 tensions rose as the Eastman and Bedel Companies each sought to assert their claims and to capture the loyalties of settlers. These people had worked hard cutting trees, clearing fields, and building their farms, and now their title was threatened. Factions rose with escalating tempers as Bedel, Eastman, New Hampshire, and Canadian factions, and shifting combinations, argued their positions.

New Hampshire also began to wake up to the fact that there were settlers on land it claimed north of the forty-fifth parallel. The legislature decided to make an example of these squatters. In late 1820 the attorney general was directed to file charges of trespass and suit was brought against two settlers. But it wasn't until December 1824 that the Eastman group, feeling its interests threatened when New Hampshire asserted its claim to Indian Stream, asked the legislature to recognize the legitimacy of its claims. The legislature, however, did not back the Eastman claims and instead passed resolutions reasserting the state's right to the contested lands.

In the meantime a boundary commission, which was supposed to settle the boundary between the United States and Great Britain, became hopelessly bogged down. The king of the Netherlands, asked to arbitrate the dispute, awarded the whole of the contested territory to Great Britain in 1831. With the award of Indian Stream going to Great Britain (and Canada), no one knew if the Canadian authorities would recognize title to anyone's land. And there still was no local government other than unofficial annual meetings held by the settlers.

The U.S. Senate rejected the king of the Netherlands' findings in 1832 by a narrow vote of twenty-three to twenty-two, and the border question came back to life. In the interim the Bedel and Eastman factions saw that the course of wisdom was to join forces and defend the claims of the settlers against New Hampshire.

On July 9, 1832, sixty men of the Indian Stream settlements met at the schoolhouse they had themselves built. The talk was of forming a government to bring a semblance of civilization to their ranks. They asserted their right to originate their own government and did so, adopting a thirteen-point bill of rights, establishing legislative and judicial bodies, and creating the Republic of Indian Stream.

The legislative body, called the General Assembly, was made up of all males twenty-one years and older who had lived in the territory for more than three months. A council of five was established to run daily affairs. The proposition was adopted by a vote of 56 to 3.

Although they had never before acted, both New Hampshire and Canada began to assert their authority in 1835. First, a New Hampshire Sheriff's deputy who tried to arrest an Indian Stream man was sent packing home. Then the Canadian claim was suddenly enforced when Magistrate Alexander Rea in Hereford, Quebec, issued a warrant for an Indian Stream man who was promptly arrested and taken into Canada. Although he was released a few days later, protests flew and tempers flared.

The governor of New Hampshire ordered the Coos County sheriff to enforce New Hampshire's laws and ordered the militia to get ready in case it was needed. On June 26, 1835, the legislature of New Hampshire voted to assert its authority over the territory. The Indian Stream Republic was dying but not yet dead. Sixty-two settlers feared the state's intervention and set about to draft a petition to Canada asking for protection. New Hampshire then ordered its sheriff to meet with the Indian Stream men, telling them that if they didn't accede to New Hampshire jurisdiction, the New Hampshire militia would enforce state law. Many reluctantly agreed in order to avoid bloodshed.

By October the Canadian government still had not responded to the settlers request for protection. Magistrate Rea decided to again issue a writ for the arrest of an Indian Stream man, this time Richard Blanchard, who had been appointed a New Hampshire deputy sheriff. Rea deputized two Indian Stream men as Canadian officers to make the arrest inside the Indian Stream Republic. The arrested man, an officer of the republic and favorable to the New Hampshire claim, was led off on foot into Canada, while his forteen-year-old son set off to spread the alarm.

Quickly a group of men was formed to rescue Blanchard, and they followed the trail of the group across the border and into acknowledged Canadian territory. Narrowly avoiding bloodshed, they managed to surround the Canadian group and secure Blanchard, then they raced back to the border.

Another group, setting out from Caanan, Vermont, then decided to capture the Indian Streamer who had sworn out the warrant for Blanchard. A group of more than fifty armed men invaded Quebec. Close to the home of Magistrate Rea, they collided with Rea's men, and the upshot was bloodshed and Rea's capture. He was immediately, and rather undignifiedly, hauled back to Caanan. Tempers were at a boil on both sides.

On November 13, New Hampshire decided to end the standoff and invaded Indian Stream with a force of two officers, two sergeants, and sixteen privates. New Hampshire's war was very much of an anticlimax. In spite of outbursts of anger and a bit of shouting and threatening, the war was short. New Hampshire had triumphed with the loss of no life and only a few injuries, none from gunshot.

Within two days, the authority of the state was established and the long festering dispute was at an end. Some of the most ardent supporters of the Canadian cause, especially those who had supported the raid into Indian Stream, slipped quietly over the border to begin again in Canada. Others either grudgingly stayed on or left for new frontiers in the vast American West. In the end only one man was charged with treason, and he ended up serving a short jail term, the only man punished as a result of the war. The Indian Stream Republic, a noble experiment in self-government among frontier peoples, was dead.

Canada didn't get around to sending a committee of inquiry until late December, and they were promptly sent home. The vexing border issues still remained until finally settled by the 1842 Webster-Ashbuton Treaty, which granted all the land east of Halls Stream to the United States and New Hampshire.

Lizzie Bourne:
A Young Life Lost
· 1855 ·

Mount Washington has been the source of a mysterious and beckoning myth from the earliest colonial times, and it drew curious adventurers to it like a magnet. In the case of Lizzie Bourne, a young and attractive woman from Kennebunk, Maine, the attraction was more like that of a moth to a flame.

Before Lizzie's visit to the mountain and even before the arrival of Europeans, the Pequawket Indians living in the shadow of the huge mountain they called Agiocochook did not climb it. They believed that it was inhabited by the gods. It was not known to have been climbed until 1652 when the adventurer Darby Field, an English settler from Exeter, came in search of mineral riches rumored to abound in the mountains.

Over the course of the following two centuries, a few groups of men sought the challenge of climbing the mountain, including the eminent New Hampshire historian Jeremy Belknap, who lead a scientific party to the summit in 1784. Agiocochook was first called Mount Washington by Belnap to honor the leader of the American army, who had retired that same year.

It wasn't until 1851 that Mount Washington claimed its first recorded victim, the son of a member of Great Britain's Parliament. Impetuous and rash, Frederick Strickland was staying at the Notch House, owned by Thomas Crawford. In late October he decided to climb the mountain and took a guide and another Englishman along with him. Together they rode by horse up the bridle trail. Encountering bitter cold and snow, the guide halted the company and recommended that they turn back, but young Strickland protested. Dismounting, he gave his horse to the other two and went on by himself on foot, saying that he intended to descend to the Fabyan Hotel after reaching the peak.

The rest of the party returned to the Notch House and arranged to have Strickland's luggage sent on. The next day, they stopped by Fabyans to see Strickland and discovered that he had never arrived. A search party set out and followed his tracks onto the mountain but lost them on the way down. It wasn't until the following day that some of his clothes and then his battered body were found in the frigid waters of the Ammonoosuc River, on the flank of the mountain.

Just four years later, the Bourne family of Kennebunk, Maine, journeyed to the White Mountains. On September 12, 1855, they arrived at the Glen House Hotel, a fine grand hotel, where they could admire an expansive view of Mount Washington. Across the road from the hotel, the Mount Washington Carriage Road led across a field and followed an old bridle path up the side of the mountain. Newly constructed, the road went only as far as the Halfway House and had not yet reached the mountain's peak.

As the morning of September 14 broke, a steady rain soaked the ground and blotted out views of Mount Washington. As the Bournes prepared for lunch, however, the skies began to lighten and the rain stopped. Looking out at the mountain, George Bourne decided to meet with his daughter, Lucy, and his niece, Lizzie Bourne, who was daughter of the judge of probate for York County. Planning their day, they excitedly decided to climb the mountain.

Lizzie was a pretty, thin, and active young woman, twenty-three years old, but she was also somewhat frail and suffered from a heart condition that worried her parents. Guests at the

Glen House, however, noticed how lively, attractive, and interested she was in all about her. She was excited at the prospect of the climb and wanted to stay at the Tip-Top House, a hotel that catered to climbers, on the summit of Mount Washington. Eagerly, she pressed her wish on her uncle until finally he agreed that they would stay on top that night so they could see the sunrise from the top of New England.

Gentlemen and ladies of the time did their climbing in full formal clothing—trousers or knickers with a dress shirt, tie, and suitcoat for men and full long skirts for women. Lizzie and her cousin wore stockings, pantaloons, several petticoats, and full outer skirts of yards of fabric, heavy to begin with, even heavier when wet. It was late in the day when they started, about 2:00 P.M., but they were light-hearted.

Setting off, they followed the carriage road toward the Halfway House, a handy spot for rest and refreshment, which they reached about two hours later. Accounts differ as to whether they stopped at the Halfway House, but all seem to agree that they met a Mr. Myers who, finding that they intended to go to the top that afternoon, vainly urged them not to try to make the trip because of the hour and expected bad weather. But they insisted, starting up the trail from the end of the unfinished road. They were sure they could reach the summit that evening.

The Tip-Top House was owned by Samuel Spaulding, and late in the afternoon two of his sons started out from the mountaintop hotel to go down into the valley. After they had gone about 2 miles, they met and exchanged greetings with the Bournes who, they reported later, seemed to be getting along fine and looked forward to spending the night on the summit.

But Mount Washington's weather is unpredictable, especially in the fall. As evening fell, strong winds started to blow, and the party became chilled as they struggled upward. They passed through the lower forest of thick conifers that protected them from the winds and then went through a forest of trees stunted by the fierce winds and weather of the mountain. Beyond that they were above the tree line, where dampness, cold, and unbroken wind attacked them.

Clouds engulfed the summit, and Lizzie began to show signs that she was not well. The women's clothes became heavier and heavier as they soaked in the thick mists that blew around them. But they struggled on. Darkness fell and they could no longer see the rough path in front of them.

Gathered closely together in the darkness they decided that they couldn't go any further because of exhaustion, the wind, and poor visibility. As the two women lay down in the path, George Bourne set about protecting his two charges. With great effort he took stones and piled them together, forming a wall to break the force of the wind. Cold and exhausted they huddled together, George rising periodically to exercise and strengthen his protective wall. It was about ten o'clock when George, checking to see how Lucy and Lizzie were faring, discovered to his horror that his niece had died. In tears the two remaining hikers spent the rest of the night unsure of their own futures.

As morning broke, George woke and started out to seek help. It was only then that he discovered the true nature of their tragedy. Taking a few steps toward the crest in front of them, they saw that the place where he had erected his little wall and where Lizzie had succumbed was only a few hundred feet from their objective, the Tip-Top House.

For hours guests at the hotel tried to revive Lizzie, but to no avail. She was placed in a pine coffin, which had been brought up for her, and taken down the mountain, the coffin slung under a pole carried by two strong men. At the base her body was examined by doctors, and their opinion was that Lizzie had died as a result of heart problems complicated by exertion and exposure to the harsh elements of the mountain. She was taken home to Kennebunk and buried in the family plot.

Her family planned to place a large monument on the mountain where she perished, but unable to do so, they placed it at her grave site. Today, a simple monument along the side of the Cog Railway tracks marks the spot where she died. Its inscription expresses the grief of her family: "She had a lively intellect and a joyous heart and strong affections and was to her kindred and friends inexpressibly dear."

How Not to
Rob a Bank
· 1859 ·

By the middle of the nineteenth century, the French and Indian War–era settlement Number 4 had become the town of Charlestown. It was a prosperous little New Hampshire farming community close to Claremont, where industry had taken hold along the Sugar River. Charlestown enjoyed its position as a major settlement on the banks of the mighty Connecticut River.

Along both sides of Main Street, large, comfortable houses sat well back from the road, some built over the site of the old stockaded fort. The quiet town had a feeling of genteel well-being. The business center of town was at the north end of this section, with its prosperous general store and the Connecticut River Bank.

Built earlier in the century, the bank was well established by June 1859 as an important part of the community, a small but imposing Greek Revival temple to the entrepreneurial spirit of the people of Charlestown. Its prestige was heightened by the services of Henry Hubbard, a former U.S. Senator and governor, who proudly served as its president.

But the night of June 10 held some surprises for Charlestown and especially for the bank. At the end of the day's business, all of the money was counted and accounted for and safely stored in the vault, located behind the banking room.

The banking room door was then closed and locked, and the heavy outer door of the bank was locked up for the night.

Bank manager George Olcott had the duty the next morning of arriving at the bank first and preparing it for the business of the day. Approaching the bank just before eight o'clock, all seemed normal. When he tried his key in the door, however, he was puzzled when the lock refused to budge. When he finally opened the door, he was alarmed to see that the door into the banking rooms had been forced and was wide open. Rushing into the banking room, he was relieved to see the vault door still closed.

Quickly he tried his key in the outer vault door only to find that, like the front door, the lock seemed stuck. This had never happened before and his concern rose. Finally, working the lock open, his worst fears were confirmed. The inner vault door had been blasted open, and all of the money that had been safely tucked away the previous night was gone.

Olcott quickly spread the alarm, calling for the sheriff and Governor Hubbard. Together they assessed the damages. Every last gold and silver coin and all of the paper money in the bank was gone.

Without delay the bank announced a reward. It would pay $500 for information leading to the return of the money and an additional $500 would be paid for information leading to the identification of the thieves. Immediately, the sheriff's men fanned out along the roads leading out of town, searching for clues.

About 20 miles east of Charlestown is the town of Marlow, at the time a little community of farmers. One of them, Horace Gee, was concerned about his neighbor, who was very ill. After sitting by his friend's bedside through the night, Horace hitched up his horse and started home at five in the morning. On the way he came across a riderless horse and buggy slowly making their way along the road. The horses were tired and sweating and had obviously been on their way for a long while.

Assuming they were a runaway team, Horace took hold of the reins and led them to his home, tying them near the road where passersby could see them.

Some time later, Horace heard the startling news about the bank robbery in Charlestown and decided to check the wandering buggy more closely. In the back he found a number of bags, and when he opened them, he discovered large numbers of gold and silver coins, wads of paper money, a fine set of burglar tools, some women's clothing, and a buffalo robe bearing the inscription "S. Barton, Jr."

Hurrying off to Charlestown with the errant horse and buggy in tow, he went straight to the bank to claim the reward. Carefully checking the contents of the bags, Governor Hubbard was pleased to have all of his money back, as well as a new horse and buggy. The recovery occurred so soon, however, that he reconsidered his haste in offering such a generous reward, telling Gee that he would be paid only $400 because the expenses of the bank had been so high.

Grumbling about being treated so poorly, Horace Gee left, leaving behind money, horse, buggy, and burglar tools. Governor Hubbard still had a problem. Who had robbed his bank and how in the world did the loot-filled horse and buggy turn up in Marlow?

No one had paid much attention when a horse and buggy drew into Charlestown at nine o'clock on the night of June 10. There was nothing suspicious looking about the man and woman on its seat as they passed quietly through town. Tying their buggy out of sight, they went to the bank and let themselves in using a skeleton key. Within three hours Abijah Larned and his brother had gained access to the bank vault and took everything they could find. Pleased with the success of their job, the two put the money in the back of their buggy and headed out of town over Hatch Hill. Once out of town, the women's clothing was discarded and tossed into the back, covering the bags of money.

With the weight of two hefty men and all that gold and silver, the horse had a hard time making it up the hill. To lighten the load the Larned brothers decided to walk, one ahead of the horse and the other behind, with the horse between them. The fast walking brother in front quickly outpaced the horse, while the slower brother behind quickly lost sight of the horse and buggy. When the brothers finally met at the top of the hill, both were astonished to find that the horse and wagon had disappeared.

Panicked, they retraced their steps downhill, finding neither a trace of the missing animal nor their cargo. By dawn's early light, they finally awakened local farmers to help them retrieve their "runaway" horse, and still they couldn't find a trace. Finally, aware that the law would soon be on their trail, they abandoned the search and escaped in different directions.

What the Larned brothers didn't know was that partway up Hatch Hill, cutting into the underbrush along the road, there was an old woods road that had been cut for lumbering operations. While it was too dark for the robbers to see the horse's tracks and wagon-wheel marks heading off the road, the tired horse saw an easier route and took it. Plodding slowly through the rough road, the hapless horse spent the entire night walking through the deep woods until found by Horace Gee.

Governor Hubbard quickly dispatched lawmen to Oxford, Massachusetts, when it was discovered that the "S. Barton, Jr." who owned the buffalo robe was a well-known bank robber who lived there. Barton had a good alibi for the time, but the two Larned brothers, who also lived in town and who were known for their criminal activity, were both missing.

It wasn't until December that the sheriff's men caught up with Abijah Larned in Utica, New York. Surprisingly, he immediately agreed to return to Charlestown without any court proceedings in New York, and after packing his bags, he left for New Hampshire with the lawmen.

In Charlestown he immediately confessed to the robbery. Contrite, Abijah apologized to Governor Hubbard and charmed him by offering to reimburse the bank for all of its expenses, including the cost of repairs to the bank. He even went so far as to reimburse the bank for the rewards that it had paid out and insisted that Horace Gee be paid the additional $100 of reward money that Governor Hubbard had withheld.

So pleased were the bank's officers with the apparent honesty of the repentant robber that they agreed to his being released on bail of $2,500 to be posted by a respected citizen of Charlestown. A citizen was found to post bail, and Larned pulled $2,500 out of his bag to repay the man and then paid the bond-poster an additional $250 in cash for his troubles. If anyone wondered where he got all the money, no one asked.

In what has to be one of the most brazen bluffs of any robber, Abijah Larned then demanded that the bank return his burglar tools to him. When the bank refused, he even threatened to sue, and, astoundingly, the bank relented, carefully returning to Abijah Larned the means to recoup the money that he had paid out in Charlestown.

Saying good-bye to his new friends, Abijah left, promising to return for the trial. He didn't, of course. He was not heard of until some time later when it was learned that he had been sent to prison in New York State for the robbery of a bank in Cooperstown. Abijah's brother was never apprehended, and Abijah was never prosecuted in New Hampshire because he died while in prison in New York.

The Impossible Railroad

· 1869 ·

A born New Englander, Sylvester Marsh and a friend, the Rev. A. C. Thompson, decided to climb Mount Washington one day in the mid-nineteenth century. On the steep slopes of the mountain, they were lost and then encountered one of the sudden and fierce storms that the mountain is famous for. Finally, just as dusk fell, they found their way to the stone bastion of Tip-Top House, a small inn, where they found a warm bed and supper.

There had to be a better way to get to the top, Sylvester mused as his toes warmed by the Tip-Top's fireplace. Then the idea came to him: Why not build a railroad to the summit of Mount Washington? Even for the nineteenth century, Sylvester Marsh's plan sounded like a crackpot idea. The road through Crawford Notch was a mere dirt path through rough rocks in 1858, yet he proposed to build a railroad to the top of Mount Washington, 6,288 feet in the air. Insane, they said.

Marsh was born in Campton on September 30, 1803, the son of a farmer. Marsh had an ambitious spirit that served him well. When only nineteen years old, he walked to Boston to work as a produce seller at Quincy Market. Moving on, first to Ohio and then to Chicago, he became a founder of the meat-packing industry. When his fortune plummeted in the economic depression of the 1850s, he began business as a grain merchant, developing one of the first popular consumer cereal products.

Retiring from the grain business in 1855, he returned to New England and, with friends, he developed the concept of operating a self-propelled steam engine using a wheeled cog gear on the engine that engaged other linear cogs that were fixed to the rails.

A working model was made, and in 1858 Marsh decided to approach the New Hampshire Legislature for a charter to build and operate a railway from the base of Mount Washington to its summit. One amused solon suggested that the charter be amended to allow him to build his railway all the way to the moon, a sobriquet that stuck. It became known as the Railway to the Moon.

In spite of—or perhaps because of—the impracticality of his request, he was granted the charter in June, with the condition that the railway be completed in five years. Because of the financial depression that immediately followed the grant and the advent of the Civil War, he was given an extension.

It wasn't until 1866 that work on his dream began, but he had not lost sight of his quest in the interim. As early as 1861, he had worked out the details of his engine and track and had been granted patents for a locomotive powered by cog gears and for a rachet device that could be used to stop the train in emergencies.

When Marsh tried to get others to invest, he had tough sledding. One railroad executive tossed out his letter, thinking it was from a crazy man. A group of nine men came up with $20,000 to begin the project, $5,000 of which was Marsh's own, and $500 of which was his son's. Nonetheless, Marsh persevered. He bought 17,000 acres of land running from the present Route 302 to the summit of Mount Washington. Marsh began to clear a path from the road to the point where the railway was to begin.

Leading a pair of oxen up the path, he took his work team to the proposed base station, which was later named Marshfield in honor of Marsh and Darby Field, the first European to climb Mount Washington. This was an untouched wilderness, reachable only by a rough path through a virgin forest that itself was accessed from a road that wasn't suitable for vehicles other than work wagons. And yet, he was determined to build a railroad.

Once begun, work progressed rapidly. Trees at the base station were cleared and a water-powered sawmill was built. Soon, the mill was turning out lumber from the felled trees, to be used for the base-station buildings and for the railway itself. When the water supply became inadequate, a steam-powered mill was installed. In May 1866 Marsh contracted for the building of the first locomotive, which was shipped, disassembled, by rail to Littleton. Ox carts then hauled it to the site, where it was assembled. They named it Hero, but it has gone down in history by the name the workers gave it, Peppersass, so nicknamed because to the workers its strange-shaped smoke stack looked like a bottle of peppersauce.

The operation of the train was simple but ingenious. Parallel rails were laid over a base of ties. In the first year these rails consisted of an iron strap bolted over a wooden strip. Almost immediately, however, conventional rails replaced the originals. Midway between the outer rails was another set of rails made of heavy angle iron. Riveted between the angle iron were heavy-duty bolts, in effect creating a linear gear. Under the engine two cog gears fit directly into spaces between the bolts in the middle rail.

The power of the engine was geared directly to the cog. On the ascent the engine pushed the passenger car up the mountain. Friction brakes and a rachet system engaging the middle track provided braking safety. On descent the engine backed down the mountain ahead of the passenger car. A brakeman on the passenger car controlled the speed of descent, using the car's own brakes, and the engine in front of the passenger car provided an added measure of safety.

By the end August of 1866, Marsh was ready to show his railroad to the world. Marsh's list of invited guests included both men and women and a host of dignitaries. Most important were the rail tycoons whom Marsh wanted to invest in his dream. The atmosphere was electric as the nervous guests waited to board this impossible railroad.

For more than two hours Peppersass pushed top-hatted and hoop-skirted state and railroad dignitaries up and down the completed lower track. Excited, the guests gathered at the White Mountain House and voted Marsh an accolade of achievement. Railroad money flowed in to assure its completion.

The railroad's path roughly approximated the trail Ethan Crawford had marked in 1833. By the middle of August 1868, the track was completed to the top of Jacob's Ladder, the steepest section where the train took to a trestle, sometimes more than twenty feet in the air and at an upward grade of over thirty-seven degrees. From the base station the train climbed about a mile on track at ground level, then traveled the rest of its journey on a series of trestles until it reached the summit. After crossing over the Jacob's Ladder trestle, it mounted the shoulder of Mount Clay and turned southeast up the shoulder of Mount Washington.

The track to the top was finished on July 2, 1869, and the railway opened to the public the next day. On opening day the first ride was free, and by the time invited guests had arrived, uninvited guests had to be removed from the cars so invited guests might have a place to sit. In its August 21 issue *Harper's Weekly*, the premier magazine of the times, carried an article about a trip to the top of the mountain on the cog railway. It had intimations of adventure, excitement, and thrills. The fare for the round-trip ride was $2.00 per person.

The wild and crazy idea of Sylvester Marsh became the public's dream trip. Marsh had succeeded, and in 1870, only a year after it opened, the railway carried about 3,000 passengers.

At first the train took almost three hours to reach the summit. Shortly, transit time was reduced to an hour and a half.

Today the trip, using engines and cars much like the originals, takes about an hour and a quarter. It is a journey back in time and a leisurely way to see the wonders of the highest peak in the northeastern United States.

The Cog Railway operates year-round, bringing visitors to the top of the northern Appalachians for sight-seeing in summer and skiing in winter. It's not an inexpensive trip, but considering the staggering cost of constantly rebuilding the trestles and rail system, it's a bargain. At the base station you can take a tour of the facility where locomotives and railcars are now made, the only place remaining that still makes steam-operated locomotives.

And if you are looking for Sylvester Marsh, he was pushed out of the limelight as his railroad investors, attracted by the 1868 demonstration, used their muscle to take over his railway. He moved to Concord, where he died December 30, 1884, and was buried in Blossom Hill Cemetery.

The restored Old Peppersass, the first engine, is on open display at the base station off of Route 302 in Bretton Woods, where it spent so many years at work.

How Concord Won the West
· 1895 ·

The old stagecoach rattled down the street. The stagecoach, its frame bereft of paint, door panels missing, and loaded with excited passengers peering from within, had survived many an Indian and bandit attack. Riding at the head of it was Buffalo Bill Cody, the famed scout. But this wasn't Cheyenne or Deadwood. The scene was Concord, on July 4, 1895, and the old Concord Coach had come home after thirty-one years of traveling around the world.

Buffalo Bill's coach was but one of more than 3,000 coaches that were made in Concord by the Abbot-Downing Company and its successors. While Bill's had been made in 1863, the tale started further back in history when Lewis Downing arrived in Concord, some say to see a girl he admired, and settled there as a carriage maker.

When he opened his shop, young Downing made hard-riding buggies with bodies fixed to their axles. He made them by hand, by himself, and they were cheap, only $60. Three years later, in 1816, he bought a six-acre parcel of land and set up a factory, employing up to a dozen men, who even did the ironwork for the wagons instead of having it done at the state prison as before.

As Downing prospered, he decided to add a chaise, a lightweight carriage with a top, and he brought Joseph Stephens

Abbot to Concord in 1826 to work on it and his plan for a coach. Abbot left after a short time, but returned in 1828 to form a partnership with Downing that lasted until 1847, when the firm split into two coach-building companies. Two years after the split, the Abbot company suffered a disastrous fire but was able to rebuild. As a younger generation of owners took over, they ended the separate lives of Lewis Downing & Sons and J. S. & E. A. Abbot, and the two firms reunited in 1865 to do business as Abbot Downing & Co.

Although the companies made more than forty different styles of carriages, wagons, and other conveyances, the most famous was their Concord Coach. The Concord Coach was available for six, nine, or twelve passengers, and in several configurations. These became the stagecoaches of the Wild West, bringing the mail through, carrying travelers from town to town.

For as long as the coach was a viable means of transportation, Abbot Downing & Co.—and Concord—were famous. The company was a major vehicle manufacturer of the time, its product sold worldwide. The few remaining company records show sales to Australia, several South American nations, South Africa, and to companies on the west coast of North America, which were establishing the communications network for the new territory.

The coach orders that the company received often called for several units—or even several hundred. In 1856 they received an order for 250 coaches from a new company, the Overland Mail Stage, owned by the John Butterfield Company. Soon coaches were being shipped from Concord to coastal seaports, where they were placed aboard clipper ships and sailed around Cape Horn to San Francisco.

Three years after the first order, in October 1859, the first mail stage from San Francisco reached Tipton, Missouri, in only twenty-three days. While Yankee-built clipper ships were making records by shortening the journey around Cape Horn, New

Hampshire–built stagecoaches were shortening the trip overland to California.

One of the proudest days for the company, its employees, and Concord came on April 15, 1868. The steam engine *Pembroke* sat on the tracks at the freight house in Concord with hundreds of people watching. On board the open freight cars were thirty coaches, painted rich red with yellow running gear. Painted over the doors of each was "Wells Fargo and Company." Just after 1:00 P.M., the train pulled out bound for Omaha, Nebraska, with four men from Abbot Downing & Co. on board with the carriages to ensure that this important new customer was satisfied.

Behind the success of the Concord coach lay not only the skill and careful workmanship of the men who made them, but the quality of the materials as well. Tough elm was used for the hubs of the massive wheels and white oak for the spokes. The bodies were crafted from oak, ash, and basswood, all chosen by the company as standing timber, cut, dried, and formed by the company to insure highest quality. Each carriage was finished with several coats of paint, then delicate scrollwork was added. Scenes depicting the locale where it was to serve were painted on the door panels and often portraits of female singers were applied to the footboards.

They were not only things of beauty, but the high standards of workmanship and materials made them tough and reliable. The huge bodies were suspended on thick, heavy-duty leather straps, called thorough-braces. These straps hung under the body to act as a spring and absorb shock. Made by another Concord manufacturer, the Page Belting Company, the straps gave the coach a swaying and rocking motion rather than a harsh jarring action as the coach rode over rough ground. Smoothing the ride saved passengers from the worst road hazards and the horses from injury as well.

Despite popular belief the Wild West wasn't the only place the coaches were in demand. From the early days of tourism in the White Mountains, the coaches were favorites with the grand hotels. Passengers were met at the closest railroad station and driven in elegantly outfitted coaches to the porticos of the finest hotels. Every hotel or inn that aspired to the "right" clientele had to have one.

Elsewhere in New England, other coaches served as a rail or bus line would today. They ran regular scheduled trips between towns on a daily basis, connecting just about every town of any size. Because the Concord coaches were built to last, they often had very long careers indeed.

For example, coach number 80 was built in 1850 and sold to a buyer in Lake Village, near Laconia. It eventually passed into the hands of Leander Sinclair, who ran the Great Falls and Conway Stage Company and Dover and Conway Stage Company, which used number 80 to bring passengers from the railhead at Milton to Conway. After twenty-three years of passenger service, the coach was sold in 1873 to the owner of the Bearcamp River House. He repainted it, putting the image of the hotel on its doors, and used it to pick up hotels guests at the station and to take them on outings. Among its noted passengers was John Greenleaf Whittier, who often stayed at the Bearcamp until it burned in 1880. Now thirty years old, the coach went to Massachusetts, where the wealthy William Emerson Baker had opened the Hotel Wellesley, in a building moved from the Philadelphia Exposition. The hotel burned in 1891, but the coach stayed on as a local attraction until it was bought by Henry Ford in 1925 for the Wayside Inn.

But what of Buffalo Bill's carriage, how did it fit into the history of Abbot Downing & Co.? It was built during the winter of 1863–64 and sent to Boston, where on February 18, 1864, it was stowed in the hold of the clipper *General Grant*. It traveled to San Francisco, one of thirty-two ordered by the Pioneer State Company. It saw its first use as a mail coach from Deadwood, South Dakota, to Cheyenne, Wyoming, one of the most dangerous routes in the west.

The coach suffered repeated attacks by bandits and by a Sioux raiding party, often escaping but occasionally successfully ambushed. Later used for the transport of gold from California, it was robbed of $60,000 in gold when outlaws took over the stagecoach station at Cold Spring. On yet another run, Calamity Jane herself took over the reins, saving the coach and its cargo. Buffalo Bill found the coach abandoned after one of these attacks and acquired it, using it in his Wild West show reenactment of "Attack on the Mail." He took it with him to Europe, where royalty admired and rode in it.

The celebration of the Fourth of July 1895 in Concord was a special one. Early in the morning, an unlikely group assembled and at 9:30 they set off down Main Street. The local newspaper reported the next day that "the crowd was dense and every piazza, stoop, curbstone, fence-top and balcony was converted into a temporary viewing stand, while standing room was at a premium all along the line."

Leading the way was the hero, Buffalo Bill Cody, graying at his temples now, but still showing the vigor that marked his younger years. Behind him rode the United Calvary of the World: uniformed American, British, French, and German horsemen carrying the flags of Britain and the United States, surmounted by a dove of peace.

The next participant was as popular as Buffalo Bill himself, the Deadwood Mail, the decrepit Concord Coach. Inside proudly rode the mayor, Lewis Downing Jr., and several of the men who had made the coach, one of whom had made the ironwork. Following the coach came a horde of Native Americans, all done up in war paint and wearing not much else.

At the end of the route, the biggest attraction of all awaited. The Buffalo Bill Wild West Show was there, with its riding and shooting exhibitions, even Annie Oakley herself. But the biggest thrill of all was the ambush of the Deadwood Mail by the Sioux and its rescue by the cavalry. The Concord Coach was the real hero of the day.

Stagecoach number 80 was completely restored in the 1970s by Edward Rowse, perhaps the best known of coach restorers, and can now be seen in the lobby of the Concord Group Insurance Companies on Bouton Street in Concord. There are several others on display in the Concord area: at the Museum of New Hampshire History, 6 Eagle Square; the Concord Monitor, 1 Monitor Drive; and Canterbury Shaker Village, 288 Shaker Road, Canterbury.

The World's Eyes on Portsmouth

· 1905 ·

One of the major ports of the United States during colonial and post–Revolutionary War eras, Portsmouth had lost much of its preeminence by the beginning of the twentieth century. But on the other side of the globe, a war for the control of Manchuria between the rising Empire of Japan and the old empire of Russia was about to bring Portsmouth back to the attention of the world.

By 1904 Russia had extracted concessions from the Chinese that gave it substantial control over most of Manchuria. In February of that same year, Japan launched a surprise attack on Port Arthur that destroyed the Russian fleet there. By the following spring, Japan had inflicted more severe defeats on Russia, eventually seizing Mukden, Darien, the Russian naval base at Port Arthur, and Sakhalin Island. Russia, to reestablish its sea power, sent its Baltic fleet to Asia. That fleet, too, was destroyed by the Japanese in the Tsushima Strait between China and Japan in late May 1905.

Russia had suffered a year of serious defeats. The effort to supply its troops was hampered by the limitation of the single-line Trans Siberian Railway. And Russia was suffering serious revolutionary threats at home. Japan, on the other hand, while uniformly victorious in battle, was beginning to feel the pain of war as well. The cost of the war was very high and the military began to realize that they had reached the end of their capabilities. Both sides needed peace and were slowly coming to that conclusion. The problem was that neither side would be the first to ask for it.

The American president, Theodore Roosevelt, was deeply concerned by the war and its potential effect on the balance of power in Asia. The United States had only recently acquired interests in the Philippines, as a result of the Spanish-American War, and in Hawaii, and he was concerned about the threat of rapid growth of Japanese power in Asia. After the sinking of the Russian Baltic fleet, the president contacted both governments, urging them to agree to a face-to-face conference. He knew the stress each was under and by mid-June had convinced the adversaries to agree to a meeting.

Rejecting European capitals and the Hague, the parties finally agreed to meet in the United States. The president thought that summertime Washington, D.C., would be too hot and too distracting, so he looked to such places as Newport, Rhode Island, and Bar Harbor, Maine, as possible sites for the conference. On June 22, 1905, Gov. John McLane of New Hampshire extended invitations to the governments of Japan and Russia to conduct peace negotiations wherever in the state they felt that conditions would be most conducive to fruitful negotiations.

Portsmouth had a lot to offer as a site. It had the relative solitude of a country resort, but the facilities of a fair-sized city. The Portsmouth Naval Shipyard was also a big advantage. If the negotiations were held at the navy yard, there would be better control of access to the delegates. The navy yard also had all of the latest communication facilities already installed. Up-to-date telegram facilities would assure the participants of rapid contact with their governments.

On July 7, the people of Portsmouth first heard word of their coming notoriety, when the *Portsmouth Herald* reported that the city was under consideration. On July 10, it became final. Portsmouth and the navy yard were to be the site and the conference was set to begin in early August.

At the navy yard the government had just completed construction of a large new brick building, intended for storage. It was now taken over and fitted out for the conference. Drapes were installed to preserve privacy, and the refitting was so well done that the Russian delegation thought it superior to their own foreign ministry buildings at home. A long table was placed over a large carpet in the center of the conference room and twelve new wooden swivel chairs with leather upholstered seats and backs were arranged around it. Telegraph facilities were installed and the room was ready for the conference.

The delegates were to stay at the Wentworth Hotel in nearby New Castle, a favorite seaside resort for the wealthy since it opened in 1867. It would accommodate more than 400 guests, and it stood on a slight hill overlooking a bay. Its large and elegant lobby, dining room, lounges, and ballroom could be opened to catch ocean breezes, and the windows were covered with mosquito netting to protect guests within.

On August 8, a small flotilla sailed up Portsmouth harbor bearing the guests. The delegates had, during the preceding few days, all been welcomed by the president at his home, Sagamore Hill, at Oyster Bay, Long Island, where he had set up his summer White House to be nearer the meeting. The Japanese were aboard the ship *Dolphin,* and the Russians were on the presidential yacht *Mayflower,* both escorted by the naval ship *Galveston,* when they arrived in Portsmouth amidst great pomp and ceremony.

The city was crowded with hordes of people, some of whom had parts to play in the upcoming conference, and many others who were excited and curious about the grand events about to unfold in their town. Included among the throngs were tens of representatives of the world's leading newspapers who were staying at the well-known Rockingham Hotel in Portsmouth.

U.S. Assistant Secretary of State Pierce and the commandant of the naval shipyard, along with Governor McLane, the New Hampshire Congressional delegation, the governor's staff, and executive council, met the delegates and had a gala luncheon at the Peace Building. After the initial festivities, the entire group moved across the river to the Rockingham County Courthouse in Portsmouth, where another grand reception was held in their honor.

Eventually, the well-greeted but tired plenipotentiaries made their way to the Wentworth Hotel, 4 miles from Portsmouth, as guests of the United States government. They settled into their rooms for what became an almost month-long ordeal of confrontation and cajoling. The rooms themselves were rather small and had simple furnishings common to seaside resorts of the time, but the common areas of the hotel were filled with Victorian elegance.

While the Japanese delegates tended to cluster together, the Russians enjoyed mingling with the other guests in the hotel and were found everywhere. The leader of the Russian delegation, Serge Witte, delighted in telling other guests small details of the negotiations. Aside from the sheer enjoyment of it, the Russians wanted to befriend the Americans so that there would be more goodwill toward their country. Neither side had faith that the conference would succeed, and the Russians wanted to make sure that any failure would be blamed on the intransigence and aloofness of the Japanese.

Each day, the delegates traveled from the Wentworth to the Peace Building. They actually had three possible ways to travel: by boat, by carriage, and by automobile. The first was the easiest and quickest for it was only a short and private ride upriver to the navy yard. But both delegations liked being seen by, and mingling with, local people along the way so they chose carriage and automobile, riding in style in Pope-Toledo cars along the roads to Portsmouth.

Throughout the long days of the conference, Governor McLane stayed in Portsmouth doing all within his power to ensure that it was a success. Anticipating the conference's success, he even planned to lead the exhausted delegates on a tour of the state, exhibiting to these world leaders, and the horde of media that followed them, the beauty of his state and the power of its industry.

The conference stumbled. Japan wanted control of Korea, the cession of the Liaotung Peninsula and the whole of Sakahlin Island, and indemnity from Russia. Russia wanted to save face and vowed that it would make no territorial concessions, nor would it pay any indemnity. President Roosevelt tried everything to break the impasse. He engaged the kaiser of Germany, the French, and even British friends in the effort. Finally, the American ambassador to Russia was able to convince the reluctant Czar to cede half of Sakahlin Island, which the Japanese had taken by force earlier. On August 29, the impasse was broken. The parties agreed to terms and the conference was a success.

A telegram to Sagamore Hill announced that an agreement had been reached and that peace had come at last. A triumphant Theodore Roosevelt released the word to the world. The following year, he was awarded the Nobel Peace Prize for his efforts in bringing the war to an end. But, alas, Governor McLane never got to take the delegates on his triumphal tour of New Hampshire. Once peace was agreed on and the treaty signed, the delegates were quickly called home and Portsmouth again receded from world attention.

As a symbol of their thanks to the host state of New Hampshire, each delegation presented to the state a gift of $10,000, in the bonds of their nations, to be used by the governor for charitable purposes. The gifts were constituted as a fund to be spent for those purposes, but alas, the Russian bonds ceased paying interest when the revolution of 1917 overtook the Czar. An interesting twist of history brought the matter back to public attention when the Soviet Union fell in 1991.

The State of New Hampshire asked the new Russian government to honor the old bonds but they were refused, probably not unexpectedly.

The Peace Building was subsequently used for submarine design and bears a plaque commemorating its key role in history, while the Wentworth Hotel, now the Wentworth by the Sea, after a long period of decline and disuse, has been saved and renovated, again taking its place as a leading seaside resort and spa. The in-town Rockingham Hotel, which housed the world's leading journalists during the conference, has been converted to other uses but still stands elegantly on State Street in Portsmouth.

Cornish: Capital of the United States

· 1915 ·

Woodrow Wilson was looking for a place where he could get away from the intense summer heat of Washington, D.C., during the summer of 1913. The place the president chose was the Cornish estate of a friend, the famed author Winston Churchill.

Churchill's estate, called Harlakenden Hall, sat on grounds that covered more than 700 acres of wooded plains and hillsides. Churchill was not alone in his rural solitude, for Cornish had attracted some of the finest writers, sculptors, and artists in the United States as summer residents. The studios of the great deceased sculptor Augustus Saint-Gaudens were there and the painter and illustrator Maxfield Parrish lived in town. It was a lively arts community, and the former university president turned U.S. president and his family enjoyed the summer in the peaceful, Connecticut River valley so much that they decided to return two years later.

The summer of 1915 was a much more stressful and crucial time in Wilson's presidency—and in world history—and Cornish became the summer capital of the United States. Great events in Europe, Haiti, and Mexico drew the attention of the world to this little village. Churchill's big plum-colored brick Georgian house was where Woodrow Wilson made decisions that would affect the world.

Britain and France were locked in combat with a German enemy that seemed all-powerful. And despite the administration's strong policy of neutrality, America was being drawn into the conflict. In late April, Germany placed ads in American newspapers warning Americans not to sail on British liners; newspapers opined that such scare tactics were in bad taste. But on May 7, 1915, the warnings gained credence when a German submarine torpedoed the British liner *Lusitania* with the loss of 1,198 people, including many Americans. The president demanded an explanation, apology, and reparations, and Germany was considering his demands. Britain, too, was a problem for the Americans because its government demanded that the United States, although neutral, stop trade with Germany.

At the same time, a rebellion in Haiti threatened anarchy, and Mexico was in chaos after the assassination of Pres. Porfirio Diaz and the revolution that followed. By 1915 Venustiano Carranza had chased the assassin Victoriano Huerta into U.S. hands, and Pancho Villa and Emiliano Zapata were each leading rebel armies on their own crusades.

In the midst of all of these tensions—and probably because of them—the president and his family returned to Cornish. They left Washington at midnight on Wednesday, June 23. Crowds greeted the train at several cities along the way, and the popular Wilson waived from the train's rear platform.

This time, direct telegraphic communication was set up between the summer White House and the Washington White House. Newspapers reported on Saturday, June 26, that Germany was expected to move against Paris, Calais, or Warsaw. But the president, in New Hampshire, rose early and took a walk in the woods before sitting down in his study to work.

By now Wilson was a grandfather, and his daughter's family was also staying with the family in Cornish. On Sundays most of the family loaded into flivers and headed off into Vermont, where they rode up through the foothills of the mountains until they became hopelessly lost. Stopping to ask directions, the driver asked, "Where does this road go?" To the amusement of the president, he received the classic Vermont reply: "I've been living here all of my life and it never went anywhere."

Victoriano Huerta, who had overthrown a Mexican president and had himself been deposed, was found in Texas on June 28. Although Wilson did not have have all of the details, he ordered Huerta arrested for trying to foment revolution in Mexico. Wilson then motored off to Hanover to play golf with his physician, Dr. Cary Grayson, as the two had often done during the 1913 visit. Ever popular, Wilson doffed his cap to well-wishers along the way. But affairs of the world intruded again when they returned. He spent the afternoon in his study, trying to force the British to allow goods of American companies shipping from European ports through their blockade.

In concert with Secretary of State Robert Lansing, the president worked on the European and Mexican problems for the next several days. While he still traveled the 20 miles to play golf in Hanover, he now spent more time in the study. Germany had sunk another liner, costing one American life. Some British vessels were flying the American flag to prevent German attack and Wilson needed to issue a protest. On Saturday, July 3, he crossed the river to play golf at Windsor, but when he returned to Cornish he learned that the former president of Mexico had died in Paris, a bomb had exploded in the U.S. Capitol building, and an attempt had been made on the life of his friend J. P. Morgan. His pleasant day over, he returned to work.

Although the president had originally planned to return to Washington on July 6, he stayed on, golfing twice that week in Cornish and Hanover. He was finding rest and relaxation, even with Germany and Mexico on his mind, and friends said he was gaining weight and looking more physically healthy. But Wilson was deeply involved with Mexican issues. Food supplies in

Mexico City were low, and thought was given to letting Pancho Villa set up a provisional government to stop the anarchy.

The president received word on Friday, July 9, that Germany had finally responded to the second American note about unrestricted submarine warfare, but he would have to wait for its transmission from the embassy in Berlin. That day, as was becoming his pattern, he played golf at Hanover in the morning, worked for a few hours, and then went on an outing by car. He broke his custom of not having official guests during his vacation and invited Gov. Rolland Spaulding of New Hampshire to the summer White House.

The next day, the president played his customary round of golf with Dr. Grayson before settling down to study the unofficial version of the German response. The response appeared unsatisfactory and cutting off relations with Germany was in the air.

Although it was rumored that Wilson would return to the capital on Sunday, July 11, he remained in Cornish, studying the official version of Germany's reply. Meanwhile, the situation in Mexico grew worse. There was no effective government, and Wilson was being urged to intervene in the name of humanity to save the people of Mexico from "bandits."

The president's almost daily golf games continued. On Friday, July 16, it was announced that he would return to Washington the following week. He played his last golf round on Saturday and returned to the White House on Monday, leaving his family behind in Cornish. The decision had been made to reject the German note, but to maintain relations, continuing negotiations.

His stay in steamy Washington, D.C., however, was short. On Saturday, July 24, he was on the train again, headed north, after telling Germany that the United States insisted on freedom of the seas. After a round of golf on Monday, the president learned that an American ship had been torpedoed by Germany. He declined comment.

The next day there was no golf. Wilson closeted himself with his stenographer after news arrived that the President of Haiti had fled to the French embassy after rebels entered and burned the Presidential palace. But the morning golf rounds began again on Wednesday. Returning to work in the forenoon, he attended a formal tea that his daughter Margaret had arranged for the afternoon for the arts and literature community of Cornish.

Wilson continued to divide his time between vacation activities and the problems of the nation. In August he ordered the invasion of Haiti to save its pro-American government, and on August 5, U.S. Marines from the battleship *Connecticut* seized Port-au-Prince. Wilson rose early to receive news of the invasion while in his study.

But Haiti wasn't the only place on his mind. The chaos in Mexico led him to decide on August 10 that it was time for force. Just after noon, he telegraphed instructions that the battleship *New Hampshire* and other naval vessels be sent to Vera Cruz, Mexico. On Wednesday, August 12, the president left Cornish for the nation's capital for the last time.

Woodrow Wilson's stay in Cornish had been relaxing, but momentous. The course of relations with Germany had been set, chaos in Haiti had been quelled, and the decision was made to restore government to Mexico with American military force—a lot of history was made in a quiet little town.

The Last Wild Drive

·1915·

What the cattle drives of the Old West were to ranchers, the log drives of New England were to the lumbermen, who saw the great unspoiled forests of northern New Hampshire as their treasure trove. From the mid-nineteenth century until 1915, log drives down the Connecticut River were an annual event. Then came the last one, a truly wild melee of water, wood, and men.

The Connecticut River starts on the northern tip of the state just above a small pond called Fourth Connecticut Lake. Gathering waters from adjacent valleys, it flows south, passing through Third and Second Connecticut Lakes before reaching First Connecticut Lake. The latter two lakes played a key role as places where logs were gathered together before the start of the wild down-river ride.

During the fall and winter, cutters took to the woods to gather and stack the timber that would be sent south in the spring. Temporary villages of log houses, or occasionally sawn boards, were established deep in the woods at the end of long dirt roads. Most often, the houses were miles from the nearest settlement and were intended as places of temporary habitation, covered on the roof and sides with tar paper and heated by a single woodstove in the center.

All winter the cut logs were hauled to a landing on the side of a stream that had been selected for its depth and the straightness of its course. Logs were stacked on gently sloping ground, parallel to the side of the stream in huge piles called "rollways." The stream was dammed to create a pond that would store enough water to carry the built-up supply of logs all the way to the Connecticut River.

Spring was the exciting time for the woodsmen. They watched the rivers like hawks, waiting to be sure that the ice had melted. Then the signal was given, and men mounted the rollways, rolling the stored product of their winter labor into the ponds behind the driving dams. Sluices were placed strategically in the dams and with a roar, the sluices were opened. The logs took off on their wild ride to the Connecticut.

When the loggers went into the woods for the fall and winter season in 1914–15, there were persistent rumors that the Connecticut Valley Lumber Company, the biggest in the area, was going to stop long log runs on the Connecticut. The rumors proved to be true. The company announced that the next log drive would be the last ever held on the river. Every woodsman in the north country wanted to be part of this historic drive.

In the fall and winter of 1914–15 more than 2,000 men were in the woods harvesting and storing up logs for the last great drive. Old loggers and young men only a few years in the woods, and the kid brothers who didn't want to miss out on the chance to brag about the experience in their old age, signed on. This was the event of the age in the north country. Then, in April the ice was gone from the lakes and rivers. The men mounted the rollways to start the drive. The huge logs began to move down from their tall piles into the water as the men on top scurried and danced from log to log, trying to keep from becoming part of the forward crush themselves.

In the Second Connecticut Lake, 40 million feet of logs shot down the river before being gathered in big booms and towed across First Connecticut Lake. In South Bay there were another 15 million feet, Perry Stream yielded 5 million, and Deadwater Brook 6 million feet more. The north woods were hemorrhaging logs.

Once they were in the water, the logs were in the realm of the rivermen, the highest paid of the logging men, and the ones with the most dangerous jobs. Rivermen were the cowboys of the log drive. They had to keep the huge, uncontrolled, mass of long and unruly logs moving. The logs, like cattle, wanted to go every which way in the rushing waters and needed constant corralling by the rivermen.

In the upper reaches of the Connecticut, before the construction of big power dams, the river flowed through rapids and over falls. Small dams erected to provide water for small mills also impeded the flow, as did numerous highway and railroad bridges. Islands dotted the river from place to place. Each of these were obstructions that could impede the great drive by causing a log jam.

The flow of logs miles long and covering the river from bank to bank came inexorably onward, scraping the banks of the river until it met an object that stopped it. When that object was a bridge, the logs would continue to press forward, compacted by the unceasing flow of the spring-swollen river. As the pressure grew, logs rose, tangled, and sometimes shot straight up into the air, all the time putting tremendous stress on the bridges. Occasionally, logs would poke up through the bridge floors, sometimes they even swept the bridge downstream.

These were the most difficult and dangerous times for the rivermen, because they had to get out into the jam, find the key logs, and loosen them while trying desperately to keep their foothold on a floating log. Their tool was a peavey, a long heavy staff with a sharp pointed tip and a hook—invented in 1857 by Edward Peavey, himself a riverman.

Out on a jumble of logs jammed together by a raging stream of water, the rivermen worked together and individually. At Perry Falls one man went out into a jam, and when his peavey touched the water, he lost his balance and fell in. Trying to save himself, he grasped at the side of a log that rolled and he slid under water and drowned. Wearing heavy boots and thick wool shirts and trousers, the rivermen had little chance once they fell into the raging stream. Few rivermen even knew how to swim.

Ice in a river can jam just as easily as logs, and when the drive reached North Stratford on the Vermont side of the river, it ran into an ice jam piled against the bridge of the Grand Trunk Railroad. This was one of the worst jams that anyone had ever seen. Stopped by the ice, logs dove into the water and rose 20 to 30 feet above it. Almost half of the logs in the drive were piled up behind the bridge. Behind them, water continued to press forward. Rising water ripped up rail tracks, and flooded houses and barns as the pressure on the railroad bridge grew.

Desperately, the men worked, prodding and pushing at logs and ice. One riverman, having carefully placed a charge of dynamite, was dismayed when the explosion had no effect. Tying charges to two more stakes, he again worked his way out into the mass and plunged the charges into a hole where he thought they would do the most good. When they exploded he flew into the air, but landed upright on a log and floated serenely downstream.

Along the course of the river, other men patrolled the banks in shallow draft boats called bateaux, pushing logs back into the stream. Others drove teams of horses that would haul logs back into the stream. It was hard work. Horses often fell, breaking legs as they clambered over rocky shores and river bottoms.

Camps for the men were set up in fields along the river, with cooks ready to serve up hot chow. Agents bought food for the men and hay for the horses as the annual procession passed by for the last time. Along the river crowds gathered as the word spread that the drive was approaching. Brave souls gathered on the bridges to watch the mass pass below. The first few logs sliding by beneath them were soon followed by an ever increasing army of logs until the water was covered with them. Other people watched from the safer vantage point of the embankments. Few would ever forget the sight.

While the drive lasted, the towns along the river celebrated, and in 1915 they did so with an appreciation that this was the last time it would ever be seen. At night, sweaty, dirty, and tired, the rivermen would gather in the saloons and bars of the towns as they passed. Young boys watched their easy and confident stride and were envious, knowing that they would never be able to join in the drive.

Too soon for some of the men, the historic drive neared its end. Big booms of logs chained together stood ready to gather and hold them until they were needed by the sawyers at Mount Tom. Down came the logs from the high north into their waiting arms, and down came the rivermen ready to gather up their pay. All of the most famous rivermen of the time were there to cash out.

While most of the men returned home to their farms with a large pile of cash, others went into a frenzy of celebration, spending most of their final pay on booze, women, and wild living. In the years that followed, many of the 1915 "river rats" continued to work on the river in short log runs; many others returned to their farms or to jobs in the factories along the rivers. The days of the great long log drives were over.

Murder and the Mountains

·1918·

At the height of World War I, the death of a popular local gentryman shook the town of Jaffrey. Soon its 2,000 residents were embroiled not only in the expected whodunit guessing game, but also in an international intrigue. Before long fissures split the town, rich against poor, Catholic against Protestant, and American versus foreigner, opening wounds that would last for years.

In 1918 Jaffrey was a small rural town whose population lived in the village center and in the surrounding hills. Mills along banks of the Contoocook River provided work for many locals, and in the summer the town's population swelled with wealthy families who came to their mountain farms to escape the city.

Like others, this town was edgy from the stress of World War I. American entry into the war had heightened anxiety and fears of German spying and sabotage.

August 13 was very hot, with no promise of any relief for the evening. Rising late, as was his custom, Dr. William K. Dean breakfasted, saw his invalid wife settled in her favorite room, and went to town to do errands. He planned to stop by the home of his best friend, Charles Rich, a banker and prominent local political figure, before returning home.

While doing his errands he ran into Georgiana Hodgkins, Charles Rich's sister-in-law, who had just arrived in town for a two-week visit. Together they rode back to Rich's house, which stood near the center of town. On arrival they found Charles with a warm compress to his left eye. His spirited horse had kicked back, he said, grazing his head. Concerned, Charles's wife, Lana, and her sister urged him to see a doctor. No, Charles said, he thought that he would be fine. Besides, Doc Sweeney had left that very day for active duty in the military and now the closest doctor was 7 miles away. After a pleasant evening of conversation, William Dean returned home shortly after 10:00 P.M. From that moment Jaffrey was never the same.

Once home, he greeted his wife and showed her his purchases and gave her a bunch of sweet peas Georgiana had sent. Hungry, he ate a few raisin buns and then announced that he was going out to milk the cows. It was almost 11:30 P.M. and Mrs. Dean sat down in her room with a view toward the barn to await his return. He never came back.

Mary Dean, then sixty-eight, had been a beautiful and intelligent woman, particularly popular among the summer people. During the preceding two years or so, however, she had declined physically and mentally, her words becoming confusing and disoriented. When her husband "Billie" failed to appear after midnight, she sat up and waited until morning before calling people in the village.

Among them were the Riches who, when they arrived after 11:00 A.M., saw her coming from the barn. Dr. Dean had not yet been found, but when Mary approached them she said, "Billie is dead," and a few moments later, "He is in deep water." All thought that her reference was to a swamp in the lower pasture, but there was no deep water there.

It wasn't long before searchers noticed a covered cistern a short distance uphill from the barn. Lifting the cover they probed with a long staff, encountering resistance. Draining the cistern of water, they lowered a man and brought up a body.

Dr. Dean was wearing a pair of short trousers with long black socks and the rubber-soled sneakers that he habitually wore when doing chores. Over his upper body was a burlap sack and the ropes that tightly bound his hands and feet were tied to it. Removing the sack, the searchers found his head wrapped in a light horse blanket and a heavy cord wrapped around his neck. There was also a twenty-seven-pound rock as a sinker.

He had been struck on the head by a blunt instrument and then had been garroted before being thrown into the cistern. The coroner's autopsy revealed that he had died of strangulation. The state's attorney general was called in and police and sheriff's deputies combed the place for clues. There were very few.

Speculation as to the identity of the assailant began immediately. Among the first suspects was Mary. Some thought her a bit jealous of Billie's friendliness with other women. Although the doctor had said, just the night before, that she was too fragile to climb the stairs or to go to the barn, she was seen doing just those things with ease on the day of the murder.

Then, too, even before the body was located, she knew he was dead and "in deep water." Or, perhaps, had the poor demented and confused woman, while sitting in her chair waiting for Billie, seen the attack and the disposal of the body? Strangely, that issue was never pursued in deference to her loss and assumed condition.

But the plot grew thicker. Mysterious lights had been seen flashing from local mountaintops and from windows of a house that Dr. Dean had rented to Lawrence and Margaret Colfelt. This "suspicious couple" were thought to be German. A local constable, under treatment for terminal illness with morphia, claimed to have seen the lights. Many others in town later also saw them. Federal agents came to town asking about the signals and about the Colfelts.

Some in town were sure that the lights were secret coded signals being sent from the Colfelt house to agents on top of Mount Monadnock and thence to German submarines lying off Boston Harbor. They believed that William Dean had found out about the spies and had been killed to silence him.

Doc Sweeney had his own explanation of the lights. Before he left town, he accompanied the constable on a sighting expedition and found some of the lights to be little more than stars and others to be auto headlights on roads over the mountains. He told the constable to stop spreading silly rumors. The issue, for him and many others, was no more than hysteria induced by wartime paranoia.

Then there was the issue of a rowdy group of young men and women who were often seen together in the dark of night. The story was about town that at night they sought out empty houses as a place of rendezvous. Had Dr. Dean found them at the empty Colfelt house, or had he encountered them—or some other intruder—in the barn?

The morning after the death, Charles Rich appeared at the bank and later at the Dean home with a black left eye and scratches on his cheek. Was his story about being kicked by a horse true? The only living witnesses to the timing of the black eye were immediate family. Dean and Rich had been together the preceding night. Had he a falling out with his best friend and killed him—or was there more to it?

Accompanying Dr. Dean's brother to Jaffrey for the funeral was Willie Wendt DeKerlor, who described himself as a criminal psychologist, but acted more as a detective. Relieved by Frederick Dean, he was soon hired by town selectmen to investigate the murder. Though German himself, he quickly became a partisan of the German spy theory and soon developed the further theory that Charles Rich, the banker, was somehow acting in concert with the mysterious Colfelts in espionage.

Rooming with the pastor of a Catholic church, DeKerlor and his two hired assistants gathered gossip all over town and spied on those who differed with his opinion. These rumors and suppositions were passed on to the priest and his housemaid and through them to the entire community.

Catholic workmen in local factories believed the spy hypothesis and thought Rich guilty. Rich's friends, the upper echelons of town, mostly Protestant, and many of them fellow Masons, knew him to be innocent. A man of his stature, position, and probity just could not do such a thing, they reasoned.

The Catholics, looked down upon by many because of their poverty and the language difficulties as immigrants, believed that the Masons were protecting their own. The dispute became one between Catholic and Protestant, upper class and working class.

As weeks turned to months, there was no solution to the mystery. Five months after the death, a grand jury was called in the shiretown of Keene. All of the major witnesses, and some not so major, testified and were examined. A printed text of the inquest runs to 350 pages of double column testimony. The jury's verdict: Murder by person or persons unknown. No one was ever charged with the death of William K. Dean.

Willie DeKerlor, discredited, was forgotten. Charles Rich, on the other hand, lay under the cloak of suspicion by townsfolk for the rest of his life, even after winning a lawsuit for libel against the *Boston American* newspaper, when they intimated that he was involved.

Mrs. Dean died only a few years later. Over time, the intensity of the controversy died down as partisans died off. But the mystery of William K. Dean's death remains and is still a matter of interest—and controversy—in the Jaffrey community.

Eight Jolly Campers
· 1919 ·

New Hampshire has long been a mecca for lovers of the great out-of-doors, and camping is among the most popular ways to enjoy it. Since the invention of the automobile, a camping trip in New Hampshire has been a favorite holiday. But few know that taking part in one of the very earliest and most unlikely camping parties of the automobile age were three giants of American Industry, one highly respected naturalist, and four others. Or that before the trip was over, Thomas Alva Edison would find himself passing the hat in Tilton, while Henry Ford, Harvey Firestone, and John Burroughs cheered him on.

Americans had known the automobile for many years, but fifty-six-year-old Henry Ford had revolutionized the transport world by making automobiles affordable. Ford pioneered the automobile assembly line, making cars so inexpensive that ordinary people could own them. But it was no ordinary camping party that Ford assembled for his trip to New Hampshire.

The eminent naturalist John Burroughs was eighty-two that year, but he was still actively searching out wildlands. He had studied nature for years and had written many books on his observations, which were often likened to those of Thoreau. That year, 1919, saw the publication of his book *Field and Study*. Burroughs himself was no stranger to camping and had done so on many occasions with companions such as John Muir and Theodore Roosevelt.

Born in 1847, Thomas Alva Edison was one of the most famous men in America by 1919. Beginning in the 1860s, he became one of the most productive inventors in American history, garnering more than 1,000 patents for such things as the electric light, the phonograph, and the motion picture projector. He also owned the Detroit Edison Company, which had hired young Henry Ford. Edison had encouraged Ford to continue his early efforts to invent the internal combustion engine. Like Ford, who had brought along his personal secretary, F. C. Kingsford, Edison also invited his business associate and secretary, Fred Ott.

Harvey Firestone was more nearly a contemporary of Ford's. Only fifty-two years old, he was one of the first to develop pneumatic tires for automobiles, the first to design low-pressure, truck, and nonskid tires. His company, started in Akron, Ohio, in 1900, supplied most of the tires for Ford's cars and was one of the biggest in the United States. Harvey decided to make the trip a family affair by bringing along his son, Harvey Jr.

No one knows exactly how this disparate group got together, but what they decided on was a camping trip that took them by automobile from Albany, New York, to New Hampshire, then on to Massachusetts. In 1919 the roads of New Hampshire were only a very rough approximation of what they have become today. Forget superhighways, these were nothing better than narrow worn paths through the woods, going from town to town. It was over these roads that the strange procession passed.

The assemblage was impressive as it set out on August 10. Two Packard sedans and an Edison Simplex carried the traveling warriors themselves. Following with the extensive camping gear and luggage was a Cadillac truck and—most important of all—a specially fitted-out Ford truck to serve as a mobile kitchen. With it came Henry Ford's personal chef, Thomas Sato.

By all accounts this was not a "roughing it" venture for this group of eight, in spite of Edison's demand that each campsite be deep in the woods. He saw to it that the cook truck included in its list of equipment a mobile electric generator that provided power not only for the cook and kitchen, but for lighting in the tents as well. The tents were carefully outfitted with screens to keep pesky insects away.

Edison was the guide for the trip, picking the route and places where the group would stay. Stopping along the way, they took to the trails. One memorable photo from the trip shows a barefoot Henry Ford sitting on a striped folding chair about to put on his hiking boots, fully attired—as a gentleman should be—in a suit, vest, white shirt, and tie. Berry picking was also high on the list of activities, the aged Burroughs and tall, thin Henry Ford intent upon the quest, both fully clothed in three-piece suits and neckties.

On August 10, the unlikely group left their campsite in the Green Mountains and crossed into New Hampshire's north country. Soon, they were headed down through Crawford Notch. Burroughs, ever the naturalist, noted in his journal how the glaciation of the mountains had left glacial erratics, he called them "drift boulders," scattered on the south facing slopes of the mountains. "The view of the White Mountains very impressive," he wrote. "We came through Crawford Notch, down and down and down, over a superb road, through woods with these great rocky peaks shouldering the sky on either side. Simply stupendous!"

The "superb road" that Burroughs spoke of was a narrow, winding trail, barely two lanes wide, that seemed barely to cling to the steep rocky mountainsides. But it was indeed superb, compared with others they used on the trip.

Continuing south, they stopped for lunch and passed through Conway, before heading west across the head of Lake Winnepesauke and south through the Weirs to Tilton. It was here that their well-laid plans came a cropper. Somewhere along the way that day, the Cadillac truck—and with it all of the tents and camping gear—became separated from the advance party.

They had planned to spend the night camping at Andover, but by late afternoon the group realized that their support vehicle had gone astray. One New Hampshire newspaper reported that they intended "to camp out in the woods over night and simply whisk through here in high gear but the straying of their equipment necessitated their seeking hotel quarters." Stopping at Tilton, they checked into the Ideal Hotel, the best place in town, with a porch from which to view the passersby.

Such a distinguished group as this would be very hard to miss, and the word of their presence spread fast. And it didn't lessen their notoriety that they chose to sit and wait for the wayward truck at one point alongside the highway, in the shade of a huge old tree in front of the library. It seems that the tree was slated for cutting by the town council, and a group of local citizens had formed to protest. In the eyes of the protesters, the sight of the famous men sitting in the shade of the venerable maple eating peanuts was an omen, and they made the most of it in their "save the tree" campaign.

Once the lost vehicle caught up with the party, it was too late to camp, and the whole party returned to the hotel in Tilton where they ate dinner, after which they retired to the porch for fresh air. Word of their plans to spend the evening in town spread like wildfire and brought everyone within reach down to the hotel. As Ford, Burroughs, and Edison took the air on the hotel's broad porches, crowds gathered and people shouted out for them to make a few remarks.

Public visits of the famous were unusual in Tilton and became moments of public entertainment. Celebrities draw crowds, and, reasoned the Franklin division of the Salvation Army, this presented an unexpected opportunity to collect a few coins. So off to the gathering they went, tambourines in hand.

Burroughs was the first to speak, saying a few nice words about the pleasure of being there. He was soon followed by the usually reticent Henry Ford who spoke in the same vein. But at this point the unexpected happened. Looking down into the crowd from the porch, Thomas Alva Edison, the famed inventor, saw the collection plate being passed by the Salvation Army followers and stepped down to the street below. Seizing the tambourine, he began to circulate among the crowd, and no one could resist him.

The presence of the great man in among them encouraged the good folk present to dig into their pockets and soon the tambourine overflowed. Edison borrowed a hat from a bystander as a supplementary vessel. Before Burroughs headed off to spend the evening with friend at nearby Webster Lake, Edison had gathered an unexpected windfall for the Salvation Army.

The *Keene Evening Sentinel* reported the next day that "Mr. Edison passed the hat and tambourine among an audience composed of everyone in town who could ride, walk or hobble to the Ideal to see him, Henry Ford and John Burroughs standing on the hotel veranda together."

Early the next day, the group motored from Tilton over to Webster Lake, before heading south again toward Keene, which they reached at about two in the afternoon. As they had done in Tilton, they headed to the best hotel in town, the Cheshire House, at the time famous for it outstanding dining room.

They were warmly greeted by a crowd, and Mr. W. H. LaHiff stepped forward and invited the famous visitors to stay over and attend the annual St. Bernard's Reunion, scheduled for the next day. But the invitation was declined. Henry, Thomas, Harvey, and John explained that they planned to get to Springfield, Massachusetts, that night. Gathering their caravan, the jolly crew headed out of town, never having actually set up their camp in New Hampshire.

When David Beat Goliath and Lost: The Textile Workers Strike

· 1922 ·

In 1805 Benjamin Prichard started a small textile mill along the falls of the Merrimack River at a place called Derryfield. Only marginally successful, he sold it to new owners, who in turn sold to a group of Boston businessmen in 1831. They called their new company the Amoskeag Manufacturing Company, a tribute to the falls that were to build an empire.

In 1810 Derryfield's name was changed to Manchester with hopes of rivaling the British city's textile prowess. This New World Manchester, in the mid-1830s, gave birth to an industry that became the largest of its type in the world. By the 1920s it had surpassed its English namesake in the production of textiles. But labor unrest was about to bring it down.

Amoskeag Manufacturing Company started with capital of $1 million, but no individual had particularly large blocks of shares in the company. There was no dominant owner to stamp the enterprise with his own mark. The stockholders, however, also owned the water-power rights for the entire

Merrimack River, and bought up 15,000 acres of land, virtually the entire area of present-day downtown Manchester.

The corporation set about planning their new city. The industrial land along the river was reserved for the corporation, including an area just uphill from the factory that was saved for company housing. Another area was established as a business district and lots were sold to approved businesses. As the factories began to flourish, so did local businesses.

House lots were laid out in other places for sale to factory workers, and special arrangements were made so that they could afford to own their own homes. Home ownership, the stockholders believed, created better employees because ownership gave them a stake in the town and thereby the company.

Most of the early employees were unmarried girls from small family farms scattered around New Hampshire and the other New England states. On the reserved slopes uphill from the mills, sturdy brick boarding houses were built, providing sound and healthy lodging. To protect their virtue and reputation, the girls were required to attend church, refrain from alcohol, and abide by a 10:00 P.M. curfew. Single men also lived in company boarding houses, while married workers were generally left to find rental property in the community or to buy their own homes.

Since ownership of the company was so diverse, it was run by its treasurer, who had offices in Boston, and by its agent, the man in Manchester who was responsible for the operations of the massive company. The agent, who was only an employee, had so much responsibility, authority, and power that many of the employees thought he owned the company.

Manchester was not a true "company town" as defined by the time. The difference was that the company did not have a company store from which employees had to buy. The company fostered many independent businesses where its employees could shop.

From the beginning of operations in 1837, the new company continued to grow. In the first several decades of its life, it invested its earnings in new plant facilities and equipment. In Manchester different groups of investors, all with interlocking directorates, started new companies, making the same or similar products. One by one these new companies were acquired by Amoskeag Manufacturing Company until all but the Stark Mills Corporation was integrated into the overall Amoskeag plan. In 1942 Stark was brought into the Amoskeag fold.

The early Amoskeag Manufacturing Company was benevolent, with many programs to improve the lot of its employees. A textile club fostered learning and encouraged employees' advancement, and there were social clubs and baseball clubs for wholesome recreation. While the company controlled the town by controlling its governing body, the Board of Aldermen, and by being closely associated with the police department, it acted paternally toward the employees, establishing parks and other public works.

After only a decade or so, the original farm girl workers were supplanted in the 1850s and 1860s by Irish families, willing to work for lower wages to escape the privations of Ireland. By 1860 there were almost 4,000 Irish in Manchester. German and Swedish workers were also becoming more common, taking many of the more skilled positions denied the Irish. Scottish weavers, who were particularly adept at gingham weaving, were recruited and brought into the international workplace mix.

Then, a few Polish workers came from elsewhere in New England, along with a few who arrived directly from Poland. By the 1870s even these sources of new workers were insufficient, and the mills began recruiting workers from farming communities in rural Quebec. First individuals and then entire families were encouraged to move to the town. Slowly, French Canadians became the great mass of workers in Amoskeag. While they never achieved the management and social position of most of the other immigrant groups, their importance arose from the shear force of their numbers.

Through World War I, the mills prospered. Demand for their product was high, with the government taking a great part of their production for war supplies. Capacity continued to expand and wages rose. It was the best of times for Amoskeag Manufacturing Company—or so they thought.

While the company originally put much of its profit into new plant facilities and improvements, by World War I management was setting aside profits, gathering up money until a stash of $30 million lay in the company coffers by 1924. More than 5 million yards of fabric were shipped out weekly. They were produced in sixty-nine buildings with a combined floor space of more than 8 million square feet, by seventy-four separate departments.

More than 17,000 workers were employed during the peak years of the company, and it was the largest integrated textile mill in the world. The Amoskeag mills covered a mile and a half on the east side of the river and a mile on the west side.

While Amoskeag prospered, it never took notice of the growing textile industry in the southern states. Wages were substantially cheaper there, and those plants had the added advantage of newer buildings. They were also equipped with more efficient machinery, and they operated the factories for three shifts. In contrast, Amoskeag's buildings and equipment were aging, obsolete, and inefficient, and Amoskeag had only one work shift a day. Furthermore, New Hampshire taxed the inventory of the mills, but southern states taxed profits instead. By the end of World War I, New England factories were hard pressed, and they responded by cutting wages and increasing hours.

The workers at Manchester felt safe because their company had protected them. So it was a rude shock on February 2, 1922, when they were told that wages and piece rates would be reduced by 20 percent and work hours would be increased from forty-eight to fifty-four hours per week. On February 13, 1922, more than 12,000 workers went on strike, shutting the company down for the first time in its history. The company announced that it would keep the mills open, but very few employees crossed the picket lines. So began the long strike that proved disastrous for both the workers and the company. The Amoskeag was the primary employer in the city of 75,000. The United Textile Workers had only started organizing in 1919, but the February wage and hour notice brought the union to the front lines of the confrontation.

Workers felt betrayed by a company they had trusted. The familial relationship between employer and employee that had lasted from the 1830s was irretrievably broken. After nine long and painful months of the strike, the company agreed to restore the 20 percent wage cut, but it kept the longer hours. Most workers returned to the fewer jobs that were then available.

In 1925 management split the Amoskeag Mills into two companies. The operating surplus, which by that time had fallen to $23 million, was divided. The new corporation, the Amoskeag Company, was given $18 million while the manufacturing arm, Amoskeag Manufacturing Company, retained only $5 million. Amoskeag Manufacturing had lost its ability to modernize its plant facilities and equipment.

From 1922 the company declined. Layoffs were frequent and wages were decreased. New strikes in 1933 brought violence, and labor trouble lingered. By 1935 the company was in deep trouble. A series of layoffs starting in March reduced the workforce from 11,000 to fewer than 1,000 by September. A temporary shutdown was announced. Then floods ripped through the mills in 1936, damaging buildings and equipment.

Company reorganization in bankruptcy court failed and on July 10, 1936, the Amoskeag Manufacturing Company was ordered to liquidate assets. The city was devastated, more than 11,000 people were already registered with the state unemployment office and thousands more sought relief. By then, many workers felt that the recent strikes had been a mistake and had ruined the company, but it was too late. And the strikes had only hastened the inevitable.

Today, the reborn mill buildings, dominating the east side of the Merrimack River, house a multitude of different manufacturing, service, and retail businesses. Tidy brick rows of former workers' housing line the streets that rise from the mills to the business district, now private homes and professional offices. The Manchester Historic Association, in a renovated mill building, has exhibits exploring the history of the mills and the resulting ethnic character of the city.

How New Hampshire Invented Skiing
· 1932 ·

All over the state of New Hampshire during the 1930s a small and enthusiastic group of outdoorsmen was learning the new sport of skiing and creating new technologies to make the sport safer and more enjoyable. But a chance meeting between an anti-Nazi Austrian and a foreward-looking ski enthusiast resulted in the creation of a school that shaped an American industry.

In the beginning the sport was the province of clubs, made up of men of primarily Scandinavian origin who gathered together for the physical activity and the thrill of organized winter sporting contests. One of the earliest clubs, Berlin's Nansen Ski Club, was formed in 1872. In addition to Nordic skiing (cross-country), the Nansen club built a ski jump, one of the first. (Burned in 1971, the jump was rebuilt as an 80-meter steel frame jump and hosted the world championship jumps in 1972.)

Another of the earliest clubs was the famed Dartmouth Outing Club, formed in 1909 in Hanover. Starting with cross-country trips in the Connecticut River Valley, members took on more activities, such as climbing Mount Moosilauke and skiing down its snow-covered road. It was at Dartmouth that many of the leaders in New Hampshire skiing were first introduced to the sport. Dartmouth held an annual Winter Carnival, and as early as 1911 skiing was an important part of the event. The outing club idea was quickly picked up by other colleges and universities, creating new enthusiasts for the sport all around New England and the nation.

During the winter of 1929–30, young Katherine Peckett, who lived in the section of Franconia now called Sugar Hill, convinced her innkeeper father that it would be a good idea to keep their inn open for the winter season. She hired two men to teach skiing on the open slope in front of the inn. It was the first school for skiing in the United States, and famed outdoorsman and journalist Lowell Thomas and Minnie Dole—who was later instrumental in establishing the Tenth Mountain Division—learned how to ski there with instructor Sig Buchmayer. The Pecketts had well-connected guests, and they encouraged their friends to take up the new sport. Many did, and the number of skiers grew.

So many people began coming to New Hampshire to ski that in 1931 the Boston and Maine Railroad started a new service, the Ski Train. The very first ski train traveled from Boston to Warner. On board this trend-setting train were Bill and Betty Whitney, who were to do much for the industry only a few years later. Trains later went to other New Hampshire towns and finally centered on the slopes of North Conway.

In the train's first four years of service, almost 60,000 passengers took advantage of it. Within the next five years an additional 175,000 rode, with fares from Boston ranging from $2.50 to $4.50. New Yorkers arrived on the Eastern Slope Express. The New York train made round-trip runs from Grand Central Station that were timed to leave Friday night and return Monday morning, leaving two full days for skiing, at a cost of $4.95.

During the summer of 1932, inspired by the Pecketts whose winter business had swollen as a result of skiers, a group gathered to cut the first purpose-made downhill ski trail in the United States. Laid out by Duke Dimitri von Leuchtenberg, an instructor at Pecketts, the Taft Racing Trail was cut on Cannon Mountain at the head of Franconia Notch. Its popularity led to the creation of another trail, the Wildcat Trail on Wildcat Mountain, in

1933. The trail has a 2,000-foot vertical drop. By 1934 there were forty-eight named specially created ski trails in New Hampshire, most of which are still in use.

Apart from that of the Pecketts, ski areas as we know them did not exist in the beginning of the 1930s. But there were enthusiasts, most trained in the outdoor clubs of colleges, who came to ski on open hillside fields and down carriage and lumbering roads, staying at small inns and guest houses for a few dollars a night.

The inn of Ed Moody in Jackson was one such place, and by the mid-1930s it had a crude rope tow. When Bill and Betty Whitney bought the place in 1936, they reengineered the tow, turning the drive wheel parallel with the ground, allowing the skier to be pulled up the hill at the end of a shaft with a handle—a Sears Roebuck shovel handle. It was the world's first overhead cable lift. Under the guidance of the Whitneys, their hill became Black Mountain Ski Area.

One of the Dartmouth-trained skiers was a young man from Boston named Carroll Reed. In 1934, while skiing on Mount Washington, he fell and broke his back. Recuperating in a hospital, he was visited by friends who had traveled to Austria on a ski holiday. Intrigued by a ski school they had seen in St. Anton, Austria, they told Reed of the new Arlberg method being taught. It allowed beginners to quickly learn the sport.

The founder of the St. Anton school, Hannes Schneider, had a great love of skiing and of the outdoors. His ski school used this unique method of teaching and had become a mecca for European skiiers. Reed was fascinated by what he heard. With the encouragement of friends, Reed set out to found his own ski school. Working with the Eastern Slopes Ski Club in North Conway, he made contact with Schneider and arranged to open an American branch of Schneider's famed ski school.

Young Carroll Reed arranged with Schneider to send his best instructor, Benno Rybizka, to Conway as Reed's chief instructor. After a brief but flashy publicity stop in Boston, Rybizka took up his job at the new school when it opened in 1936. The first year, operations were set up on an open pasture slope in Jackson and four young men were selected to be trained first as the advance guard of instructors. In spite of a poor snow winter, more than 6,000 lessons were given that year by Rybizka and his newly trained instructors, all in strict accordance with Hannes Schneider's system.

When Reed met banker Harvey Gibson, president of Manufacturers Trust Company, he told him about his ski school. Gibson's daughter had spent the entire first winter at the Jackson school, and Gibson suggested that Reed move the school to Lookout Point in North Conway, which Gibson had just bought. The name of the ski area was soon changed to Cranmore Mountain.

The first ski slope on Cranmore had been cut in 1936 by a group of high school students for the owner of a small inn, Kearsage Hall. The students widened and cleared an old road and set up a snack bar for skiers. After Gibson bought the land, the south slope of the mountain was cut for a trail, and Carroll Reed moved his rope tow and his ski school, opening in the season 1938–39. Reed then sold the school to Gibson.

But in 1938 Adolf Hitler had succeeded in carrying out his *anschluss* with Austria, incorporating it into the Third Reich. Hannes Schneider, an outspoken advocate of democracy, was immediately imprisoned by the Nazis as an enemy of the state. For months Harvey Gibson negotiated with officials of the Reich, and finally in 1939 Schneider was allowed to come to the United States to "visit" his friend Gibson. Hannes remained in North Conway the rest of his life.

Another problem plagued Harvey Gibson in 1939. Harvey wanted a better way for skiers to get up the mountain than the little rope tow that Reed had brought to the hill. He met with George Morton, a local man with a reputation as a brilliant mechanic, the man who had earlier built and perfected the tow at Black Mountain. The solution Gibson and Morton came up with was the skimobile, a series of little cars that ran along an elevated platform. George Morton designed and supervised its construction and even made the little cars in his automotive garage. The platform was on a trestle and was pulled up hill by a cable underneath. When it opened, it was a sensation, the first in the world, and it was copied at the Homestead Resort in Virginia. The skimobile even became a popular summer attraction.

In 1939 the new ski area at Cranmore Mountain combined the elements that were needed to bring thousands of new enthusiasts into the sport of skiing. Gibson had created specially made trails on the mountain and had developed and installed the wildly popular skimobile to take skiers to the top of the trails in comfort and ease. Thousands of new skiiers flocked to North Conway and learned the sport. They brought their friends, who in turn brought their friends. Local inns that had once depended solely on the summer trade now had business through the winter and into spring.

New Hampshire's development of skiing in the 1930s set the patterns on which the postwar American ski expansion was based. Travelers can still enjoy these historic skiing experiences at ski areas around New Hampshire. You can learn more about New Hampshire's role in the creation of skiing at the New England Ski Museum at Cannon Mountain.

The Big Blow
· 1934 ·

At 6,288 feet above sea level, Mount Washington is the highest mountain in the entire northeastern part of North America. There is no taller mountain to the west until the Cascade and Rocky Mountains on the west coast of the United States. Mount Washington is the tallest northern peak of the Appalachian Mountain chain, which runs along the eastern seaboard like a wall.

In terms of weather, what this means is that all of the winds and weather of Canada and the western United States pass freely over the continent, only to pile up against Mount Washington when reaching the east coast. Because of this the mountain has some of the worst weather in the world, and when the wind raced across the top of the mountain in 1934, it set a world record.

Even the first European explorers were aware of Mount Washington. Giovanni da Verrazano reported seeing it as he cruised along the coast of Maine in 1524. Native Americans feared climbing it, and although Darby Field climbed it in 1652, it remained unexplored into the nineteenth century, an age of inquiry and exploration. The advancement of science and technology was sudden and almost compounding, and Mount Washington's unique climate was increasingly interesting to adventurers and scientists.

Early scientific explorations of the mountain took place in 1840, and in 1854 Nathaniel Noyes spent one hundred days on the summit recording temperatures. In 1853 Gen. David Macomber, one of the builders of the Mount Washington Carriage Road, urged Congress to install a full-time observatory at the top of the mountain, a farsighted request that was ahead of its time.

Although the first hotels on the summit were built in 1852, the summit was not occupied during the winter because harsh weather conditions made resupplying materials impossible. The first successful attempt to mount a long-term scientific presence on top of the mountain came in the winter of 1870–71.

The state of New Hampshire had appointed Charles H. Hitchcock as state geologist in 1868. His job was to conduct a geological survey of the state, but in the end he became focused on the possibility of using a permanent station on the top of the mountain to predict weather. In a preliminary effort Hitchcock and a team of men wintered at the top of Mount Moosilauke during 1869–70. The following year, Hitchcock gathered a team of four others to help in his work. This time, Hitchcock wanted to make his observations on the top of Mount Washington. He convinced the owners of the newly finished Cog Railway to allow him to use their barely completed mountaintop terminal and, at his own expense, gathered together all of the supplies that would be needed for the winter.

He also convinced the U.S. Army Signal Corp to loan him the wire and equipment necessary to set up telegraph communications, and by the end of October 1870, the station was ready for occupation. When they settled in for the winter, his group had established the first high-mountain weather observatory in the United States. The U.S. Signal Service continued to operate the station through 1892, when it was abandoned.

It wasn't until forty years later that a weather station was reinstituted under the control of a group of private individuals who saw the need for the station. Joe Dodge was not only the hut master of the Appalachian Mountain Club, but he was already a legend in the White Mountains. Bob Monahan was a freelance writer and a friend of Dodge's. Together, they talked the U.S. Weather Service, the New Hampshire Academy of Science, Harvard University, and a few others into supporting their plan to reestablish the weather center.

Originally working as volunteers, in 1932 they formed the Mount Washington Observatory, a private nonprofit organization to make weather observations and conduct scientific research and testing at the top of the northeast. Only two years after the organization was formed, the observers experienced the highest land wind ever recorded on earth.

Usually by the time April rolls around in New Hampshire, the weather has warmed a bit, and aside from an occasional storm, snow is melting away. Not so on the top of Mount Washington. Passing clouds, and even moisture in the air, are hurtled against the rocky top of the mountain. When temperatures fall, the tremendous cold and winds often freeze the water and moisture into thick deposits of ice, called rime ice, on every exposed surface, even during the month of August. Rime ice coats not only rocks, but buildings, support wires, and instruments as well. It will even form on men's exposed beards, hair, and clothing.

April 11, 1934, started clear and bright but a bit cold. Although it was more than 80 miles away, people in the observatory could see the Atlantic Ocean to the east. As the day wore on, the morning conditions deteriorated, and before noon the summit was covered with clouds. Temperatures plummeted and rime formed fast on exposed surfaces, creating strange unworldly shapes.

Three people manned the observatory that day: Alexander McKenzie, Wendell Stephenson, and Salvatore Pagliuca. They worked in shifts, staying on the mountain five or six weeks at a time before having five days off. The building they occupied was made of railroad ties bolted to the bedrock of the mountain, and it was thought to be safe from anything the mountain would throw their way. Huge chains were drawn up over the top of the roof of the building and secured by bolts driven into the rock of the mountain.

In the afternoon wind velocities continued to grow alarmingly. By dark they reached over 130 miles per hour and the crew was fully alerted. The men began to think about whether they would run out of food or heat. They also worried about whether their instruments would survive the storm. Snow, wind, and cold blasted them as day became night.

When the next day dawned, winds were assailing the summit at speeds measured at around 200 miles per hour. As the three looked out the windows at the raging storm, the crew saw the window glass bending in and out, an inch in each direction. Outside, as they watched, a weather vane at the end of the cog railway line began to spin so fast that it rose, unscrewing itself and crashing against other equipment. The rime ice was building up fast, in some places as much as three feet thick. By the time the storm was over, the ice was so thick on the observatory building that the observers were convinced that the thickness of the ice was all that had saved the building from being blown away.

Pagliuca, in spite of the winds, went to break off ice that was threatening to damage the anemometer, an instrument used to measure wind velocity. As he went out, the wind ripped his parka out of his storm clothes and crushed his hood against his face. Returning to the safety of the building, he found that the winds had reached 229 miles an hour while he was outside. A short while later, the crew was astonished as they calculated the speed of the wind from the anemometer. On April 12, 1934, on the top of Mount Washington, the wind reached a measured speed of 231 miles per hour. It was the highest wind speed ever recorded on the land surface of the earth.

Salvatore Pagliuca was sure that no one would believe the numbers that he had recorded, so he decided to have the instruments that he had used tested. In June of that year, he took the anemometer down from its mount and brought it to the U.S. Weather Service in Washington, D.C., for testing. There, scientists discovered that the anemometer was slow. It took a wind of 12–15 miles per hour to get it turning, so that its reading, if anything, would be on the low side.

In 1980 the observatory moved into new quarters built on the summit by the State of New Hampshire. You can visit the observatory staff there during the summer or go to their Weather Discovery Center on Route 16 in Conway at any time of year. Exhibits and hands-on demonstrations examine not only this story, but the mystery of weather on the mountain and elsewhere.

Disaster from the Sky

· 1938 ·

New Englanders watched the sky with increasing trepidation as the weather deteriorated. Rain that had begun on Tuesday, September 13, 1938, continued all week and throughout the weekend. It had turned the entire region sodden, and by Tuesday, September 20, word of flooding was reported in newspapers. But a worse disaster was about to devastate New England and there was no warning.

In the White Mountains of New Hampshire, there were landslides and roads were washing out. Near Keene, water began to overflow roads in low areas. A Keene weather observer reported from his Summit Road home that he had recorded a rainfall of 3.89 inches during the preceding forty-eight hours. New England had suffered catastrophic flooding as recently as 1936, and here, only two years later, conditions were approaching, and exceeding, those of 1936.

When daylight broke on Wednesday morning, the city of Keene found itself awash and completely cut off from the rest of the world. Rivers were still rising, and families and businesses were scrambling to save their belongings as flooding continued to engulf low areas. The Red Cross was mobilized. Blankets and mattresses were brought to the state armory for people driven from their homes who sought refuge there. Washouts and high flood waters made travel out of town impossible. More than thirty streets were under water. It seemed as though Keene and the entire valley were about to fill with water.

Along with Keene, nearby towns of Hancock, Nelson, Harrisville, Dublin, and Marlborough had lost power; telephone service was unavailable throughout the region. Then it was announced that all train service was cut off. The nightly milk train to Boston got only as far as Fitzwilliam, a small town only a few miles south of Keene, before being stopped by a landslide across the tracks. Buses trying to go to and from Keene were unable to do so.

Police in Keene were busy. About midnight on Tuesday they helped Harold Barden by rowing him in a small boat from his house to his store on Church Street, so that he could move his goods to higher shelves. About the same time the Cummings, Lovely, and Houghton families had to be rescued from their Pike's Alley homes. Local businesses were working hard to remove equipment to higher floors ahead of the rising waters. It seemed as though things couldn't possibly get any worse, but they did. Much worse.

It began unnoticed, halfway around the world. In early September shifting winds over the Sahara desert moved westward. By September 10, the wind was a storm near Portugal's Cape Verde Islands. It then crossed the Atlantic, traveling west and growing in intensity, until about the 19th. Then, off the coast of Haiti and the Dominican Republic, it shifted north, passing Florida the next day, reaching Cape Hatteras on the morning of September 21.

By now the storm was a fierce hurricane, and a combination of tragic circumstances was about to bring disaster. The fall equinox brings with it the season's highest tides, and the equinox fell on September 21 that year. In the north a lingering high-pressure zone sat over Canada's Maritime Provinces, holding a warm, water-laden, low-pressure mass over New England. Once the hurricane turned north, weather observers expected it to blow out to sea. But they didn't account for the Canadian high, which kept the storm moving straight north.

Once in motion, the chain of events was relentless. Originally, the storm had a forward motion of about 25 mph. But once it reached the warm, wet low-pressure area off Cape Hatteras, the storm began to strengthen. The storm's forward speed then increased to more than 60 mph. Its arrival in Long Island and New England coincided with the high tide. Suddenly, an abnormally high tide, pushed by hurricane force winds of about 100 to 150 mph, struck the coast with a force so strong that it registered on seismographs in Alaska.

Sweeping across Long Island, it smashed into the Connecticut and Rhode Island coasts just as workers were leaving for the day. The storm surge instantly flooded the streets with cold sea water. The devastation in its path was horrendous. Relentlessly, the storm raged forward, finding the Connecticut River valley and following it northward. In Blue Hill, Massachusetts, winds of 186 mph were recorded, and in places the storm dropped two inches of rain per hour.

As the winds hit the coast, the people of New Hampshire had no idea what was headed their way. In mid-afternoon the storm reached already flooded Keene and the destruction of the city began.

Keene sits in a narrow valley about 20 miles east of the Connecticut River. Among its many successful industries at the time were chair factories, shoe factories, and textile manufacturers. Its broad streets were lined with huge ancient elms, the same trees that ringed its town square. It was a prosperous and community-minded place with several beautiful wooded parks shaded by tall pines.

As winds approximating 90 mph reached the city, the hour-glass shaped elms along its streets began to sway. Their roots deep in the water-saturated soil weakened, and one by one they began to topple, uprooted by the ever more powerful winds, bringing sidewalks and parts of streets with them.

Down they went around Central Square, along Court Street and West Street. On the west side of the city, nearly all of the tall pines in Wheelock Park and Ladies Wildwood Park tumbled into a tangled mass, more than 2,000 in all. In both parks it appeared that almost all of the trees had been carefully uprooted and laid out in rows.

But the damage to property was also huge. At Keene Normal School, a school for teachers (now Keene State College), many roofs were damaged and the school was forced to close for a week to clean up. At the head of Main Street, the tall upper steeple of the First Church was torn loose and, upside down, smashed through the roof of the historic building, protruding into the nave below.

Tall and heavy trees fell onto houses, crushing roofs of some and tearing others to pieces. Scores of cars and other vehicles were destroyed by falling trees and poles. The city's gas and electric plants and telephone communications were shut down and isolated by flooding. The city was now without power and unable to communicate with the outside world.

Falling trees all over the city also made travel impossible. Trees were down everywhere across streets and roads. Fire, police, and rescue workers first had to clear lanes through trees laid across highways, some trees with trunks as thick as four feet in diameter.

On Mechanic Street the three-story brick building housing Sargent's Garage had stood for many years, but on that Wednesday afternoon the winds removed the roof and top floor, heavily damaging the second floor. Flood waters rose even higher as more roofs, garages, and outbuildings were smashed into scrap. The two top floors of the Carey Chair Plant were destroyed, and there was heavy damage to the Princess Shoe Factory and the Faulkner and Colony textile plant. Hundreds of workers would be out of work until restoration of the buildings could be completed.

In Keene alone more that 225 people had to seek refuge

from the storm in shelters because of damage to private dwellings from the winds and water. The water supply was disrupted by broken mains. Huge sections of the city lay under water, and few homes had heat or water. Normal rainfall for September was 3.49 inches; that September it was 11.09 inches, 7.27 inches falling between September 19 and 21.

Keene and Peterborough suffered the greatest damage from the storm of any place in the state, but the damage elsewhere was also horrible. The Jacob's Ladder section of the Cog Railway was blown away, and forests full of trees were laid low. It was estimated that more than ten million feet of logs were on the ground, enough for ten years of building.

In Weare raging streams tore at river banks, tumbling entire houses into the torrents. Three women were swept off a bridge to their deaths. In Peterborough, already flooded before the winds, power lines were downed, igniting buildings in the flooded downtown business district and burning most of it, including the town's newspaper. In Manchester the 350 female employees of the Works Progress Administration Sewing Project on the third floor of a factory building escaped death by minutes when the roof blew off and walls collapsed just after they had left. Another Manchester factory also lost its entire upper floor, and flooding and downed trees damaged homes and blocked highways.

Between September 13 and 21, 1938, New Hampshire sustained more than $50 million in damages, at a time when oranges were two dozen for thirty-three cents, two pounds of hamburger cost twenty-five cents, and a new house could be built for $6,500. Throughout all New England, the damages were staggering. Federal aid alone exceeded $340 million. New England learned a lesson and federal flood control projects began almost immediately, especially at Keene, where the Surry Mountain Dam finally controlled the wild Ashuelot River.

Submarine Down! Death and Resurrection of the *Squalus*

· 1939 ·

Ever since colonial times Portsmouth has been connected to the sea and shipbuilding. Its ships were among the best produced anywhere. On May 23, 1939, however, the city, and the country, were shaken when one of the newest and most modern examples of more than two centuries of Portsmouth shipbuilding sank to the bottom of the sea off the Isles of Shoals.

In May 1939 there were two newly built submarines tied up at the docks of the Portsmouth Naval Shipyard. The *Sculpin* had been completed a few months earlier and had finished her sea trials. Nearby, the new *Squalus*, hull number 192 painted on her bow and tower, was only three weeks away from sea trials to test whether the submarine and crew were ready for active duty. Her 310-foot keel had been laid in October 1938, and the *Squalus* was launched eleven months later.

Commanding Officer Lt. Oliver Naquin and other officers, noncommissioned officers, and enlisted men arrived early to see how she was put together and to begin to learn how to make this huge machine respond to their instant command.

Her crew totaled fifty-seven officers and men, all fully trained submariners and most with years of experience.

Squalus displaced 1,450 tons. On the surface she was powered by four 1,600-horsepower diesel engines, enabling her to cruise at sixteen knots. Underwater she switched to electric motors powered by 126 lead-acid batteries, each of which weighed 1,650 pounds.

The oxygen required to operate the diesel engines was provided by a large 31-inch-wide vent that opened high in the conning tower above the deck. The vent also provided fresh air to the crew when the sub was on the surface. At the top of the vent was a large valve, the induction valve, always closed from within the control room when a dive was ordered.

During her tests almost all parts had worked well, and the crew was coming together into a cohesive unit. In her berth-side dive the big air-induction valve had failed to open after she resurfaced, but it was removed, disassembled, and reinstalled and had caused no new problems. Other minor problems were soon cleared up.

On May 22 *Squalus* went out for additional tests, and after a long day she returned, anchoring in a cove at the mouth of the Piscataqua River. The following morning, she headed back out to sea for a speed test to see if the crew could get her 50 feet below water in less than a minute. Lieutenant Naquin took his ship toward the Isles of Shoals, a rocky outcrop 6 miles from the New Hampshire coast. When they were 5 miles southeast of the Isles of Shoals, he ordered the sub to maximum speed and then gave the order to dive.

Every man below had a specific job to do. Those not assigned to operate the ship were stationed near critical equipment, taking notes and timing operations with a stopwatch. Naquin dropped down from the conning tower, the hatch sealing behind him, as the bow of the ship started below the surface and the diesel engines stopped. The lever to close the big induction valve was pulled, and crewmen looked at the signal board to make sure that there were no red lights blinking indicating a valve open to the sea. All was in order and the dive was about to be completed in the targeted time.

Suddenly, the unthinkable happened. The radio operator heard screams from the engine room. The sub was filling with seawater. In a flash orders were given to blast the seawater from the ballast tanks. Still she settled, then seemed to rise a bit by the bow. Then, sickeningly, she settled downward by the stern, coming to rest on the continental shelf in 243 feet of cold Atlantic water.

Water spurted from ventilation tubes and toilets began to shoot water in reverse. Frantically, the crew set about closing valves. First, the regular lights blinked out and then even the emergency lights dimmed and went out. Heroically, men threw switches to prevent explosions of battery gasses and wrestled bulkhead doors shut against the rising water. It was 8:40 in the morning and the crew found themselves on the bottom of the sea, cold and in a desperate position.

Naquin contacted the forward torpedo room and found no flooding, everyone was safe. Even though he knew that there was little chance of survivors in the engine room, he tried to contact them, but there was no answer. He tried the aft torpedo room and again there was no answer. Still, he couldn't be sure that there were no survivors. He took count and found that he had a total of thirty-three men in the three forward compartments of his ship. Knowing the wait was going to be a long one, he ordered the men to rest and not to talk, to conserve oxygen. He knew carbon dioxide would build up quickly in the sealed hull and ordered a carbon dioxide absorbing compound spread on the decks.

The order was given to fire an emergency flare in case there were any vessels on the surface in the vicinity and then the marker buoy was released. Bright yellow so it could be better seen on the grey sea, its connecting cable contained a telephone hookup. Now all that was left was the waiting.

Without word, concern was rising at the navy yard, and at 11:00 A.M. Adm. Cyrus Cole went down to the docks where *Sculpin* was about to cast off. Quickly *Sculpin* got new orders, go to sea and try to find *Squalus*. *Sculpin* quickly made her way to where her sister ship had dived but found no trace. Crisscrossing the area, the sub searched valiantly but found nothing. Suddenly, a sailor squinting against the rough seas thought he saw the dark outline of a flare, actually the sixth fired by *Squalus* that day. *Sculpin* quickly found the marker buoy, hauled it on deck, and tied it to a cleat. Contact was made but just as Lieutenant Naquin was about to report his situation, *Sculpin* rose on a wave and the cable parted. *Squalus* was lost again.

By now Admiral Cole, commanding officer of the navy yard, was aboard the *Penacook*, an old tug headed out to the scene. Also on their way were the *Falcon* from New London, Connecticut, the heavy cruiser *Brooklyn* from New York, and the heavy-duty sea-going tug *Wandank* from Charlestown Navy Yard in Boston. *Wandank* was equipped with a large 10-foot-tall diving bell, designed by Lt. Comdr. Charles Momsen.

Immediately upon arrival, *Penacook* began to make sweeps over the area with a grapple, trying to find the missing sub. Marker buoys were set out in a pattern to enclose the area where she lay. Finally, at 7:30 in the evening, the grapple grabbed hold.

Momsen himself was also on the move. A long-term Navy veteran, he personally had experienced the tragedy of submariners trapped in a sunken ship, and for a short time had been trapped below in his own ship. In spite of official lack of interest, he had developed the Momsen Lung as an escape tool and had developed an escape system, using a diving bell that could be lowered to the deck of a sunken sub. He was in charge of the *Squalus* rescue operations.

When *Falcon* finally arrived at 4:00 A.M. on the May 24, Momsen went aboard. Soon, a diver was on his way down the cable that *Penacook* had attached to the sub. At the depth at which the *Squalus* now lay, it was mind- and body-numbing work, but at last cables were attached to the platform over the forward escape hatch. Finally, after many difficulties, the huge green diving bell was lowered.

When the rubber seal on its bottom grabbed, seawater was forced out of the diving bell and it was bolted to the sub. The hatch was opened and seven men clambered on board. The sub was resealed and water was readmitted to the base of the bell, then the chamber rose along its cable. The time-consuming process was repeated twice again with more men, then it went down for the last load.

Naquin and the remainder of the crew climbed aboard, but part way up another disaster struck. The cable on the bell started to fray, threatening to doom the eight survivors and the bell's crew of two. Gingerly, Momsen and his crew raised the balky device using air pressure and guiding the fraying cable with their hands. When they finally grappled the diving bell and secured it to the *Falcon,* they had but one slender strand of the cable left. Momsen and his inventions had worked. It was the first successful rescue of submariners.

Several months later *Squalus* was raised and towed to Portsmouth with great difficulty. The remains of twenty-two of her trapped crew were recovered and one was never found. On July 30, 1939, a memorial service was held for the crew at Little Boars Head at which the Boston Symphony Orchestra, led by Arthur Fiedler, played.

The ship was decommissioned on November 15, 1939, and was completely rebuilt, including the replacement of the faulty induction valve that had caused her to sink. On May 15, 1940, she was again commissioned under the name of *Sailfish*, almost a year from the date of her sinking. Five members of the original crew were reassigned aboard the *Sailfish*.

She served in the Pacific throughout World War II with *Sculpin*. *Sculpin* was sunk in November 1943, but several of her crew escaped and were captured by the Japanese. In December, *Sailfish* located a Japanese aircraft carrier and sank it. In a terrible twist of fate, the captured members of the *Sculpin* crew were on the carrier. Only one survived.

Finally decommissioned in 1945, the superstructure of *Squalus/Sailfish* was removed and installed as a memorial on the mall at Portsmouth Naval Shipyard where it remains today.

A Village of Prisoners

· 1944 ·

In World War II a group of German soldiers found themselves only 20 miles from Berlin. But it wasn't their own capital in Germany, it was Berlin, New Hampshire. The residents of the little town of Stark were as surprised to see the enemy soldiers in their midst as the Germans were to find themselves transported to this wilderness.

Although in a rural area, farming is not prevalent in Stark. Instead, many earn their living in the woods cutting timber, particularly cutting pulpwood for the paper industry. In the early 1940s the paper industry was dominated by the Brown Company in Berlin, a small city where the paper mill ruled the town, much as Amoskeag Mills had dominated Manchester in earlier years.

During the Great Depression of the 1930s, the federal government set up a Civilian Conservation Corp (CCC) camp in town with bunk houses, dining facilities, and staff housing. Young men from all over the east coast came to build trails and other projects in the White Mountain National Forest. But, after only a short while, the camp was closed, abandoned, and forgotten.

It was the Brown Company that first approached the federal government about using prisoners of war as laborers to cut pulpwood. They would pay the government for their labor, helping to offset the cost of their care, and the prisoners would be paid in scrip, kept in special accounts for them. Stark, with a population of fewer than 500, found out about the POW camp when a group from the army came to town with Brown Company officials and took a walk around the old CCC camp in mid-January.

The camp lay alongside Route 110, the only primary road through town and only 2 miles east of the village center. Within weeks people saw workers fixing the roofs on the old barracks and erecting tall wire fences and guard towers at each corner. Across the street from the camp, barracks were built for army guards. No one asked for the townspeople's opinion and concern grew about the effect that the camp would have on the town. In full operation the camp would have a prisoner population of about 250, more than half the population of Stark.

In late March and early April, guards began to arrive, and in April the first train load of one hundred prisoners arrived and marched off to the camp. Townspeople stood silently by, curious and a bit apprehensive about what would happen if any escaped. Almost immediately, the prisoners were divided up into teams supervised by a civilian foreman and guard and marched off to the forest to cut wood.

Most of the men assigned to cut wood had never done this type of work before. It was hard and dangerous work, sorely taxing their strength and endurance. There were no chain saws; they used axes and two-man saws to do the cutting. Quotas were set, each man was expected to cut a cord and a half of wood each day. Actual production was much less, sometime as low as a half cord. The prisoners became disgruntled and the Brown Company upset.

In the summer they worked in the heat, surrounded by voracious mosquitoes and tiny flesh-eating black flies, returning to camp at night exhausted and drained. Rain storms drenched them as they worked in deep mud. In winter they went out into the woods regardless of the temperature, sometimes as low as minus ten degrees Fahrenheit, and in snow so deep that they feared not being able to run fast enough to avoid being struck down by a falling tree. Prisoner morale plummeted.

After a few months the original camp commander, a World War I veteran and a man with no sympathy for the prisoners, was relieved and a new commander, Capt. Alexandium Korbus, appointed. Korbus took immediate measures to bring the reluctant woodcutters into line. He set a quota of one cord for each man, and if the quotas were not met, he cut the rations proportionally. If only a half cord was cut, the worker would receive only half his ration. Korbus began Sunday work hours to make up the shortfall. Grudgingly, men who didn't want to work began to produce more and production rose until quotas were being met. Full rations and privileges were restored.

The guards, too, had a problem of knowing how to react to their charges. Some treated the prisoners poorly, while others treated them fairly. Soon after Korbus arrived, prisoners began to see that when a complaint was filed against a guard, it was taken seriously. Slowly, relations between the guards and the prisoners improved, in spite of the army's nonfraternization policy.

As 1944 turned to 1945, both sides began to see each other in human terms. Civilian supervisors were seen as teachers by the prisoners. The Americans' concern for the prisoners' welfare was recognized. In their turn the prisoners recognized the growing respect that each side had for the other. Small craft items and works of art were given by prisoners to supervisors and to guards to acknowledge their acts of humanity. Some few members of the community who were able to interact with the POWs came to appreciate the prisoners' insecurity and loneliness.

The men's work took them deep into forests that were sometimes great distances from the camp. They worked in rugged terrain, on hillsides that were almost clifflike, and places that were wet and muddy. They learned to use horses to skid logs, and they became experts at swinging an ax and pulling in tandem on a two-man saw. Once, when one member of a two-man saw team was taken off ill, a guard put down his rifle and helped a prisoner on the saw so that his quota would be made. Out of such small acts and growing respect, a bond grew between prisoners, guards, and a small town.

When the people of Stark first found out about the camp, they feared that escaped prisoners would take over their homes and harm them. In a strange way the fear of escapes that the townspeople harbored were tempered by the escapes that did occur. Working in the woods, some prisoners did manage to walk away but they were nearly always captured immediately. People learned that the escapes were more a matter of a need for freedom than from any thought of returning to Germany or the war. They also learned that they were not in danger from the escapees.

Often the escapees were looking for no more than a chance to be free for a while. They would get to a point where they needed to sneak off to a quiet spot just for a moment of solitude. One afternoon, a resident saw two strange men in his yard and invited them into the house. The three men sat down for a long talk while the owner's son scooted out the back door to fetch the authorities. Local sheriffs and police became used to picking up the runaways and bringing them back to camp. They would be spotted walking down the roads or passing through fields, taking little care to avoid being seen.

While most merely walked off their jobs in the woods, one pair dug a tunnel more than thirty feet long before they were discovered. Another made his escape good and was free for more than a month. He made his way to New York City, where he supported himself by selling drawings and paintings. Caught because of a chance encounter in Penn Station with a Camp Stark interpreter, he said he had to escape because the rough work would ruin his hands for painting.

The allied victory in May 1945 didn't close Camp Stark. The armed forces still hadn't released enough men, and the

Brown Company urged President Truman to maintain the camp a bit longer. A February 1946 date was set but then extended. It wasn't until May that the Germans finally left the camp, just over two years from the date of their arrival.

The 1946 parting was marked by friendship, sadness, and promises of continued contact. Several of the men preferred to stay in the United States but were forced to return to Germany. Eventually, five of the Stark prisoners emigrated to the United States and Canada and became citizens.

In September 1986, as the trees on the sides of Stark's mountains took on their brilliant autumn colors, the people of Stark again came face to face with their prisoners, this time as long lost friends. More than 1,000 people turned out to see the five German men who had come back. After a formal greeting, they met for an elegant dinner served in the town hall and then traveled 2 miles up Route 110 to reminisce.

The camp buildings are now long gone, taken down after the war and sold as salvage lumber. Today, the camp is covered with small trees and brush, and there is little to mark the story of what happened there. A state historical marker stands along Route 110 east of town, marking the spot where enemies became friends.

New Hampshire Picks a President

· 1952 ·

Since 1952, New Hampshire—with one of the smallest bodies of voters in the country—has led the way in choosing the winning candidate for the presidency of the United States. It was a chance change in a law in 1948 that turned New Hampshire into the nation's "president maker."

The U.S. Constitution doesn't say a word about how candidates for federal office are to be chosen. It doesn't say because political parties were not contemplated by the framers. It was left to the parties themselves to determine who would get to run for office under their banners. The result was ultimately a convention of party leaders where a few kingpins met in small rooms, cigars alight and drink flowing, to argue out the terms of a deal that would name the candidate. Everything was secret, and rumors abounded of unscrupulous and corrupt practices.

By the beginning of the twentieth century, much of the public was sick and tired of the heavy influence of political bosses and the corruption that such power brought. It was time for a change, time for the people themselves to have a voice in candidate selection. The solution that came to mind was a primary system, allowing followers of each political party to vote for delegates to national political conventions.

New Hampshire, one of the early states to do so, enacted a primary system in 1913, first used in the presidential campaign of 1916. Under the scheme, almost anyone could enter his name (women didn't yet have the vote) as candidate for delegate to the national convention. Well-known people entered their names and each candidate for delegate could also note whether they were pledged to a particular candidate for president.

By the end of World War II, however, people in New Hampshire were dissatisfied with the way the primary system was working. Political bosses still dominated because at the national convention unpledged delegates could bargain their votes, trading for special benefits for their states or for promises of high office in the event of victory. When the public voted in the primary, there was no certainty that the elected delegates would back the candidates the voters favored.

It was dissatisfaction with the nomination process in the 1948 presidential election that led to a historic change. Speaker of the New Hampshire General Court, Richard Upton, entered a bill that called for a "Presidential Preference Poll" to be held at the same time as the election of delegates to the national conventions. During the legislative session of 1949, Upton's bill passed. The first time it would be used would be Town Meeting Day, the second Tuesday of March 1952. That was to be a historic day.

The other part of the forthcoming political revolution also happened prior to the elections of 1948. The colorful and popular former north country woodsman turned political figure, Sherman Adams, was elected governor of New Hampshire. His election affected not only his own future but also that of the commanding officer of the forces of the North Atlantic Treaty Organization (NATO).

Gen. Dwight D. Eisenhower was a hero to Americans of the 1940s. He had commanded the Allied Forces that destroyed the Nazi tyranny in Europe, and he was made head of the forces that were holding back the spread of the Soviet-style Communism. While a few people had tried to interest Eisenhower in a presidential race in 1948, the drive had petered out with his refusal to entertain the idea. He preferred to stay on with NATO. But in 1952 things were to change, and the secret of success was to be Speaker Upton's 1948 legislation.

Governor Adams was one of the earliest to climb on the Eisenhower campaign wagon. In the spring and summer of 1951, then-Congressman Norris Cotton and Republican National Committeeman Robert Burroughs went to Paris to try to convince Eisenhower to run in 1952. Both were rebuffed, but nicely, and when they returned home they reported that they thought that the door was still open.

One key issue, however, was whether the general was a Republican. As a military man he had kept mum on his political preferences. Governor Adams wrote to the county clerk of Abilene, Kansas, Eisenhower's home town, only to find that the general had never voted there. Adams met with other key national supporters of "Ike"—Senators Henry Cabot Lodge of Massachusetts and James Duff of Pennsylvania. Lodge, they decided, would travel to Paris to meet with Eisenhower.

Ike's political position was so unknown, however, that the Democrats of the state also thought that he would made an unbeatable candidate. Roderick MacKey, the vice chairman of the Grafton County Democratic Party, decided that he would force Ike's hand by filing nomination papers for him in the Democratic primary. Things were definitely coming to a head.

In Keene, at a December Eisenhower for President dinner, Senator Duff said he knew for a fact that Ike was a Republican and that the party should hasten to bring him on board as their candidate. Governor Adams met with Lodge and told him that he had to get a definite statement from Eisenhower. Was he a Republican and would he run? Lodge went to Paris in January and came back with answers. Yes, he was a Republican. He had no intention of resigning his position with NATO, however, nor would he be involved in any preconvention campaigning, but, he recognized the right of others to nominate him at the convention.

The news was electric. The New Hampshire primary was only two months away, and the general's backers had to gear up the campaign and motivate the electorate, all without the physical presence of the candidate. On January 11, the governor filed his candidacy papers as a delegate to the convention "favorable" to Eisenhower, and within a few days he filed a nominating petition for Eisenhower. Adams then called his forces together for a grueling push.

Also filing for the presidency was Robert Taft, a nationally known conservative Republican leader, and Gen. Douglas MacArthur, leader of the war in the Pacific, whose sacking by President Truman in 1951 had weakened the president's chances of reelection. Taft was a tough opponent and his campaign was well organized. Although MacArthur withdrew his name before the election, his early presence added complexity and confusion to the mix.

On the Democratic side of the ballot, things were also heating up. Most pundits expected that the sitting president, Harry S Truman, would be a shoo-in for the nomination. But Tennessee's Sen. Estes Kefauver, who had made an attempt for the nomination in 1948, decided to try again. Kefauver enlisted the aide of major Democrat party leaders, and buoyed by his prominence in major televised organized crime hearings in the Senate, he led his coonskin-capped followers to a 19,800 to 15,927 victory over Truman in New Hampshire. A month later, Truman announced that he would not run for election.

Throughout the cold winter months, the governor and his troop of Eisenhower supporters rushed about the state, often chauffeured by the intrepid Rachel Adams, the governor's wife. Frequently, the governor would be at one rally, while Rachel and others attended another in a different part of the state.

Pro-Eisenhower and pro-Taft sentiments clashed everywhere, and while the Taft supporters had a live candidate in the territory, the Eisenhower supporters were left to tell their man's story by themselves. "I Like Ike" banners, buttons, and posters began to appear everywhere. In later years, the election took on the illusion of inevitability, but in February 1952 the outcome was anything but certain.

Finally election day, Tuesday, March 11, rolled around. This was to be the first presidential primary of the year, and it was the first in the nation in which there was a chance for voters to directly note their preference. It was a cold and windy day throughout the state. Here and there, a few flurries of heavy wet snow fell, and observers were surprised by the heavy voter turnout. More than 136,500 people voted, a number more than 50,000 higher than the previous record. Eisenhower received 46,661 votes, Robert Taft 35,828. Gov. Sherman Adams had pulled it off. The absentee candidate was on his way to the presidency, and in almost all presidential elections since 1952, the ultimate winner of the presidency had won his party's primary in New Hampshire.

Governor and Mrs. Adams continued to work hard on the Eisenhower campaign and were a critical part of his capturing the nomination at the convention and the presidency itself in the general election in the fall. Recognizing the hard work and stamina of his early promoter, the new president made Sherman Adams his chief of staff. Adams served as Eisenhower's right hand until June 1958.

Free Speech:
A Governor, a
University President,
and a Newspaper
· 1964 ·

Republican political leaders of New Hampshire have long been known as very conservative, often with a limited view of the meaning of the term *free speech*. But in 1964 a liberal Democratic governor adopted the conservative position and lost out to a university president who stood his ground. At issue was whether a Communist should be allowed to speak at the University of New Hampshire. He spoke and the hulabaloo swelled the crowd to more than 700 people.

This was not the first time that the issue of speakers had come to a head at the university. In all of these confrontations, the players all remained the same: the governor, the president of the university, and the state's only statewide newspaper, the conservative Manchester *Union Leader*.

In the contentious 1950s, the governors were the conservatives Wesley Powell and Lane Dwinell, and the university president was Dr. Eldon Johnson (and university Vice President Dr. Edward D. Eddy Jr.). During the fight in the 1960s, the governor was Democrat John W. King and the president was Dr.

John W. McConnell. The newspaper, spearheaded by its vocal publisher William Loeb, remained the same.

The 1950s were a time when the Soviet Communist takeover of Eastern Europe and the attempt to overthrow the government of Greece had raised fears of Soviet subversive activity in the United States. A Hampton man, Herbert Philbrick, published a book called *I Led Three Lives*, detailing his membership in an American Communist political cell and his role as an FBI secret agent.

The whole of Europe seemed ready to fall when one by one all the countries of Eastern Europe fell under the domination of the Soviet Union. The United States, Canada, and nations of Western Europe formed the North Atlantic Treaty Organization (NATO) to provide a common defense. The specter of aggressive and rampant Communism loomed large.

Under the influence of this dark cloud, investigations were initiated all over the United States to determine the presence of spies in American governmental, political, and social agencies and organizations. The United States Congress's House Un-American Activities Committee, led by Sen. Joseph McCarthy, conducted televised hearings on infiltration of federal agencies. Many states had their own investigations. In New Hampshire the investigation of subversion was undertaken by Atty. Gen. Louis C. Wyman.

In 1950 the University of New Hampshire trustees adopted a "controversial speakers" policy that set guidelines to deal with speakers at the university who might raise public eyebrows. The policy affirmed the school's commitment to the rights of free speech and assembly. The policy, the school said, would "protect and encourage these rights, limited only to their use under the rules applicable to all members of the university generally, and provided such free speech and assembly is not inimical to the provisions of the Constitution of the United States and the Constitution of the State of New Hampshire."

In 1954 Dr. Paul Sweezy, an advocate of socialism, was

invited by G. Harris Daggett to speak to a humanities class that Daggett was conducting at the university. After the class Attorney General Wyman conducted a probe of Sweezy's talk. He wanted to find out what had been said. Sweezy refused to tell him and was hauled into court to answer questions. He refused to answer the questions and was found in contempt of court, but the conviction was overturned by the United States Supreme Court.

Sweezy was again allowed to speak at the university in 1956, causing an acrimonious outcry from the state government and William Loeb's newspaper. In 1958 the American Association of University Professors acknowledged the university for its defense of academic freedom. Governor Dwinell, an ex-officio trustee himself, objected to the acceptance of the award, as did the attorney general, the state Executive Council, and the *Union Leader*.

During an April 1961 civil defense drill at the university, sixteen students refused to participate and, despite strident demands by Governor Powell and the *Union Leader*, President Johnson refused to expel the recalcitrant students. For three months Powell and the newspaper attacked the university for its "eggheadism," while Johnson dealt with what he saw as devices for "political assassination and educational assassination, for guilt by association, and for trial by newspaper or public investigation."

The ground was all set, then, when a student group calling itself the No Time for Politics Committee invited James Jackson, the editor of *The Worker*, the news organ of the Communist Party of the United States, to speak at the university. In the *Union Leader's* edition of April 6, 1964, publisher Loeb attacked, asserting that "Free speech should not be granted to those who want to destroy it."

Governor King, on the same day, released a copy of a letter that he had earlier sent to President McConnell when it had been proposed that George Lincoln Rockwell, leader of the

American Nazis, and Gus Hall, leader of the American Communist Party, speak to the students. In the letter Governor King objected to the use of tax-supported facilities by those by "those who publicly espouse principles that attack the very foundations upon which this country was created," and he extended that belief to the speech by Jackson.

The attorney general was asked to determine if state law would allow a Communist to speak in the public facilities of the university, and the school's chapter of the conservative Young Americans for Freedom objected as well. The governor went to the school and told the students that they could hire an off-campus hall to listen to a speech by anyone they wanted to listen to, but they couldn't use tax-supported property to listen to such "vermin." He then called upon President McConnell to ban the speech, saying that the matter was a simple choice "between what we call academic freedom and common sense. And I choose to take the road of common sense."

After King's speech the No Time group withdrew its invitation to Jackson, and the newspaper claimed a victory for the governor. Not everyone agreed with the outcome, however. Other state papers chided the university for failing to uphold freedom of speech and assembly and about one hundred students protested at the state capital in Concord, some even meeting with King in the historic Executive Council chamber. He tried to downplay his position, saying that it was limited to extremists and not to people like the Socialist Norman Thomas or the right wing leader Robert Welch. The students didn't buy it.

The school's president himself appeared before a faculty and student assembly on the same day and denounced criticism of the university for personal or political motives. During his remarks he announced that the student philosophy club, the Socratic Society, had requested permission to invite James Jackson to speak and that he had directed the dean of students to approve the request, without any conditions. The gauntlet had been thrown down.

While the faculty and students cheered his courage, the *Union Leader* carried a big editorial headline "UNH Campus Open to Reds" and excoriated McConnell and the school. The "silly students," it said, were "so stupid they can't see the difference between honoring and supporting the Communist Party, which wants to destroy freedom, and supporting the great Western tradition of allowing dissent from unpopular sources." He then warned that the newspaper, legislature, and voters would not forget.

In spite of the tirade and threats of the newspaper and the vocal opposition of the governor, President McConnell and the university held their ground. On the 24th of April, eighteen days after the first outburst, James Jackson spoke to a crowd of almost 700 people who were curious to hear what the controversial speaker would say. At the beginning of the month, most had probably never heard of him, but by the end of the month the headlines had made him a celebrity.

One observer later noted that "A university, as a place to exchange ideas, should be subject to no outside interference. We need nobody to censor what we see or hear; when the day comes that Americans cannot distinguish between right and wrong, then it will be too late . . . to do anything." He then added, "Either we're for free speech, or we're against it—there is no half-way position."

Not in Our Front Yard

· 1973 ·

On November 27, 1973, New Hampshire newspapers announced that the Olympic Oil Company planned to build a huge oil refinery in Durham. The people of the state, and particularly those in Durham, were shocked. Plans called for a monobouy system for the off-loading of oil at the Isles of Shoals, a rugged set of small rocky islands 6 miles off the coast. Oil would then be pumped through underwater pipes via Rye to the refinery on Durham Point, a 3,000-acre pristine wilderness area on Great Bay.

The new plant would have a daily capacity of 400,000 barrels of light crude oil. Peter Booras, spokesman for Olympic Refineries, estimated that more than 2,500 jobs would be created during the construction phase, and 1,000 permanent jobs would come with the operation of the plant and its associated facilities. The cost of the new facility was expected to be more than $600 million.

New Hampshire's economic problems made the prospect of employment a ray of hope for many. The Organization of the Petroleum Exporting Countries (OPEC) had recently formed and fuel prices were rising alarmingly; there was even talk of gasoline rationing. Gov. Meldrim Thomson and his staff were enthusiastic about the project, and they wanted it off the drawing boards and on the ground as soon as possible.

But opposition to the plan galvanized immediately on its announcement by the governor. On the day following the release of the plan, it was disclosed that Olympic Refineries was owned by the Greek tycoon Aristotle Onassis. People began to wonder why all of the secrecy had surrounded the project, why town officials had not been consulted or even contacted, and what would be the refinery's effect upon their towns. Thomson had met with representatives of Olympic in June, but not a word had been uttered publicly or to town officials until late November.

In Durham an ad hoc citizens group called Save Our Shores (S.O.S.) formed almost overnight, and within days it was meeting to plan ways to defeat the proposal. People in Rye, a beach town, tried to figure out its effect on their town's tourism industry. Others along the short 18-mile coast, wondered about the larger implications of having the world's largest oil refinery in their front yard. As the S.O.S. spokesman Michael Lamson put it, "The refinery would spell doom for the seacoast area's rural character since it would occupy the last large undeveloped area bordering on Great Bay."

Environmental concerns bothered many. In October the governor had asked the University of New Hampshire to study the impact of a refinery. The University president made it clear that the study would be unbiased. Booras and Olympic official Constantine Gratsos both assured the public that the plant would be nonpolluting.

But it was not particularly reassuring to the public when Booras told the press that the company did not intend to do any new environmental studies but planned to use existing environmental information. New studies, it was said, would slow down the project.

Governor Thomson, a vocal supporter of local rights, assumed that the benefits of the refinery would make it popular with a majority of citizens. Constantine Gratsos reported to the press that if there was substantial opposition to the plant the company would cancel the project immediately. If not in New Hampshire, he indicated, it would be built in Maine or Massachusetts.

On Thursday, November 29, Booras and Gratsos appeared at a meeting in Durham with town officials and citizens. "You must forget about the old style of refinery," he said. "This refinery will be absolutely free of pollution." He compared it with refineries in New Jersey and said the new plant would be nothing like that. As the meeting progressed, questions were shouted by the 150 attendees, and some officials stalked out of the meeting, upset with the shouting match that had erupted.

Clearly, even this early, things were not going as smoothly as Governor Thomson had planned. A team of real estate firms was hired by Booras to contact landowners and obtain purchase options on the needed land. Public Service Company of New Hampshire, then building its own high-profile and controversial nuclear power plant in Seabrook, worked with Booras to speed up the refinery project.

The project required a variance to the Town of Durham zoning ordinances, but no application was filed. Aside from a hearing in late November, there were no discussions with the town. Booras and the Olympic spokesmen continued to ply the press and the governor's staff with outlines of the plan, but there were few specifics.

Although the refinery was huge, Olympic pressed the point that it would hardly be noticed, and it would produce very little pollution. They did admit, however, that it could be expanded in the future. They also admitted that there would probably be a consequent development of related petrochemical industries around the refinery.

In Durham the opposition was gaining strength. A panel of town officials and technical experts addressed an audience of 350. One participant, a professor of chemical engineering, said that while there might be some appropriate place in the state for a refinery, Durham did not fit the criteria and called the refinery "preposterous." Although the chief selectman took no position, he repeated that he had been assured by the governor that there would be no interference with the town's land use controls and that the state would not seek to override its zoning. He had been reassured that a zoning change, requiring a vote of the town, was needed to build the refinery.

A petition in opposition to the refinery was circulated and Dudley Dudley, the Durham legislative representative, was chosen to present it to the governor. It was 288 feet long. But when she presented the petitions to Thomson in his office, he accused her of creating a media stunt and told her to leave. He would give the petitions serious consideration, he told the press.

In the meantime plans for the Isles of Shoals hit a snag. Although the company did get a reluctant option on the small five-acre Lunging Island, the owners of the biggest islands, Appledore and Star Islands, refused to sell an option and were adamantly opposed to the proposal.

On Wednesday, December 19, Onassis himself, together with a group of experts, came to the state, flying over the proposed sites before meeting with the governor in Concord. Opponents were angered by what was called Onassis's "arrogant" aerial view of the land and refusal to meet with the townspeople. A poll late in December showed that 65 percent of those polled rejected the refinery regardless of how clean it might be.

When the legislature met again in January, House Speaker George Roberts weighed in. There were no laws regulating refineries in the state. He filed a bill to do that, establishing a siting commission to protect the public interest. Another legislator, however, proposed an amendment to Roberts's bill that would give the new commission authority to override local zoning. After all, the argument went, a benefit to the entire state shouldn't be prevented by the selfish interest of a small town. A principle that New Hampshire citizens hold dear was now at stake.

The governor also mistook the power of the opposition. "As we get colder," he said, "I think you will find the outcries of the environmentalists will subside." In January 1974 it was discovered that the state's laws would allow most of the value of the refinery to escape property taxes, blunting one of the heralded benefits. Then the Army Corps of Engineers found the Isles of Shoals terminal to be unsuitable. The governor put on another push, extolling the plan's benefits. Local officials were taken on tours of other new refineries, and Olympic hinted that it might help Durham pay for a new sewage system.

Late in February, when a model of the refinery was unveiled in Concord by Olympic and the governor, Durham smarted from the rebuff. The governor stated the he wanted a statewide referendum on the plan and urged all towns to place the issue on the warrants for their upcoming town meetings. Through his legal counsel, Thomson said that the refinery was too important to the state to be left to home rule. Tempers flared. So much for home rule.

Finally, town meeting day arrived. Around the state several towns did have the item on their agendas and results varied; there was some support for the idea in some places. But in Durham the people had heard enough. By a vote of 1,254 to 144, the refinery was trounced. The very next day, the New Hampshire legislature rejected the bill that would overturn local zoning and voted to regulate any refinery.

Governor Thomson expressed his disappointment, but Olympic wasn't as nice about it. "The amount of abuse showered on us was incredible," one official said, accusing the people of the state of lacking sufficient maturity to decide whether a refinery was needed and whether environmental concerns could be met. Perhaps, but perhaps that is exactly what they did.

Judges in Jeopardy
· 2000 ·

Wwhat a legislature wants to do and what a state's supreme
court says it can do are not always the same. The process of
judicial review inevitably pits one branch of government
against the other, and the result can get pretty nasty. In 2000
the New Hampshire Supreme Court decided two cases that
angered the New Hampshire legislature, and the judges nearly
paid with their jobs.

Feuds between the legislature and the court go back as far
as the eighteenth century, when the legislature tried to legislate
a new ending to a case the court had already decided. In the
nineteenth century the courts had been abolished several times
as newly elected legislators tried to replace judges appointed
by their defeated predecessors. It wasn't until 1901 that the
present court structure was established, and it lasted through
the whole of the twentieth century.

But the organizational stability of the court during the
twentieth century didn't mean that the conflict had ended. A
series of cases during the latter 1990s brought relations
between the legislature and the courts to an all-time low. The
anger and hatred of the court by legislators boiled.

In 1997 a case was filed by the City of Claremont and
other towns against the state, seeking a finding that funding for
public education was a state responsibility. Up to that point it
had been solely that of the towns and cities. The court found
the state responsible for providing all students with an ade-
quate education under the state constitution. The legislature

was outraged at what it considered to be the court's usurpation of a legislative function.

The following year, the legislature passed a law requiring that county sheriffs be responsible for security in all state courts except the supreme court. Fifty-one court officers who would have been fired as a result of the law filed a suit challenging the law. The court found the new law unconstitutional as a violation of the separation of powers clause of the state constitution. Again, there was outrage in the halls of the legislature.

Already the court's budget was under attack by annoyed legislators because of the school funding case. The decision about security issues raised their anger further and set the stage for a constitutional confrontation of major proportions. This time the justices of the supreme court themselves became the target of the legislators.

The constitutional crisis started innocently enough when Supreme Court Associate Stephen W. Thayer filed a divorce action in the superior court. When a decision was issued by the trial judge, Thayer disagreed and appealed the case to the supreme court. What happened next ignited the fire. The supreme court, all of whose members had been working side by side with Thayer, could not hear the appeal of a fellow member, so they excused themselves from hearing the case and met to assign superior court judges to sit as supreme court judges to hear the appeal.

In February 2000 all five of the justices, including Justice Thayer, met in the court's large conference room to discuss the replacement panel. After some discussion, Thayer was finally sent from the room to the adjacent hallway. Chief Justice David Brock followed him into the hall and allegedly spoke with Thayer about choices of justices to be assigned, allowing Thayer to reject one of them. When the clerk of the supreme court found out what had happened, he spoke with several justices of his concerns about the propriety of Justice Thayer's involvement in the decision-making process and reported the judge's actions to the Judicial Conduct Committee. He also reported them to the attorney general, who began an investigation.

The investigation opened a Pandora's box for Chief Justice Brock and the other justices, but it was more like a candy box for the court's enemies in the legislature. A legislative investigation was called for, in addition to the attorney general's investigation, and hearings were scheduled.

When the attorney general announced that he was about to bring the Thayer matter to a criminal grand jury, Thayer, on March 31, agreed to resign his office as associate justice rather than face a criminal trial. But, the attorney general reported, he had also discovered that the supreme court had regularly allowed judges who had recused (excused) themselves from cases because of a conflict of interest to offer comments on the very cases from which they had removed themselves. He felt this should be brought to the attention of the legislature.

Allegations also surfaced that in 1987 Brock had called a superior court judge who was then hearing a case involving a state senator as a party. Brock was alleged to have made sure that the judge knew that the party was an important politician. Then, during testimony in the legislative hearings, Brock was asked about his call to the superior court judge and about certain documents, which he denied having in his possession. While testifying about the Thayer divorce issue, he also denied having met with Thayer in the hallway.

The New Hampshire House of Representatives held its investigation through early summer, and on July 12, 2000, the Judiciary Committee recommended to the full House that articles of impeachment be issued against the chief justice. During the impeachment investigation, Brock apologized to the House for his errors of judgment but maintained adamantly that he had not committed a wrongful act and had not acted out of malice or ill will. But the ill will of the House was too much for him to overcome and articles of impeachment were voted against him.

The charges against him alleged: that he had improperly called the superior court judge and had failed to tell the other judges about the call when the case was appealed to the supreme court for hearing there; that he had improperly met with Thayer and the other recused justices in February and had allowed Thayer to influence deliberations on his own case; and that he had lied to the Judiciary Committee during his testimony by denying that he had a certain letter, by denying that he had specific documents, by denying the hallway conversation with Thayer, and by denying the call to the superior court judge.

Impeachment, being somewhat like an indictment, meant that the matter was sent to the New Hampshire Senate for trial. The senators would act as the jury and members of the House would present the evidence for conviction. On August 21, the first impeachment trial in New Hampshire history took place as the six House managers formally knocked on the door of the Senate chamber and then proceeded to the rostrum. The chair of the Judiciary Committee read the charges to the standing senators while they solemnly listened. The trial itself opened several days later on September 18.

The hearings were televised and broadcast live throughout the state. For three weeks witnesses for the House and for the defense appeared and gave testimony before the Senate. Brock's very truthfulness and integrity were on the line as witnesses appeared and testified about the questioned events.

Brock maintained that he did not intend the wrongdoing alleged, and that the alleged lies were the result of a difference of recollection of events, some of which had occurred thirteen years earlier. As to the conversations with Thayer, Brock's lawyers argued that while they were probably misguided, they were a result of a long friendship and not from any desire to give Thayer an advantage in his case. Although wrong in retrospect, they were understandable and not chargeable wrongdoing, the defense stated. At the end of testimony, one of the articles of impeachment was dismissed.

On October 10, 2000, the New Hampshire Senate finally voted on the impeachment of Chief Justice David Brock. A two-thirds vote of the twenty-two participating senators was needed for conviction on each of four charges. After more than five hours of deliberation and votes on each of the articles, no article received more than five yes votes and the charges failed. The chief justice was saved. Although many were shocked by the conduct that was revealed by the testimony, Sen. Burt Cohen probably summed up the failure of the charges best when he explained: "For us to convict there must be serious misconduct . . . poor judgment is not enough."

Chief Justice Brock stayed in his post and continued to be the lightning rod for legislative–court battles until he retired at the end of 2003. Debilitating battles over the court's budget every two years and a flood of court reform bills have become the legacy of David Brock's impeachment agony.

A Symbol Slips Away
· 2003 ·

In the northlands of New Hampshire, a strange collection of granite rock lodged on the edge of a cliff poised 1,200 feet over the valley floor of Franconia Notch. Immense layers of granite extended out into the air, held in place only by the immutable laws of physics and the herculean efforts of a small group of men and women who loved what these rocks stood for. The rocks formed a natural gigantic sculpture of the face of a man named The Old Man of the Mountain.

From the first, even though people who examined him could see that he was in constant danger of collapse, he seemed immutable, a symbol of the strength of character that the people of New Hampshire saw in themselves. "Oh, I know that he will fall some day," they said, " but not in my lifetime."

Some 10,000 to 12,000 thousand years ago, when the last glacial age was ending, a process began on a shoulder of Cannon Mountain that would result in the formation of the Old Man. The heavily fractured granite rock there began to fall away. Harsh mountaintop weather, freezing rain, and snow gathered in the crevices of the cracked stone, pushing pieces out and down the 1,200-foot cliff. But it wasn't until 1805 that anyone noticed what these natural forces had created. That summer, as a crew of workers labored in the annual task of repairing the road through Franconia Notch, another pair of men were making a survey of the land in the Notch. Some say it was Nathaniel Hall of the road crew who looked up from a small lake at the foot of the cliff. Others say it was surveyor Luke Brooks who looked up and saw what no other man had ever recorded. Overhead hung an immense natural stone profile of a man's head. Excited, the road crew ran over and stood in silence, staring at the profile high above them. One thought that it looked like the current president, Thomas Jefferson.

But the onlookers also noticed that to see the profile they had to be in the right place. If they moved very far, it disappeared and became just a rocky cliff. Strangely, even though Native Americans had lived and traveled in this valley for thousands of years, there was never any legend in native lore about the stone face's existence.

Over the years the profile acquired many other names: the Great Stone Face, Old Man of the Mountains, the Profile, and simply the Old Man. But his official name was The Old Man of the Mountain, symbol of the state and beacon of the north country.

When the great orator and statesman Daniel Webster visited the profile in Franconia Notch, he was deeply inspired. "Men," he wrote, "hang out their signs indicative of their respective trades. Shoemakers hang out a gigantic shoe, jewelers a monster watch, and dentists a gold tooth; but up in Franconia Mountains God Almighty has hung out a Sign to show that in New England he makes men."

New Hampshire people, almost to the last man, woman, and child, came to see The Old Man of the Mountain as representative of their self reliance, toughness in adversity, and steadfastness of purpose. The natural phenomenon was an inspiration to many other over the years. Songs, poems, and stories immortalized the Great Stone Face.

Viewing the Old Man quickly became a goal of summer visitors from around New England and beyond. As more people came into the valley to see it, more hotels were built, including, in the mid 1860s, the famed Profile House at its foot. The original Profile House proved too small and was torn down. It was replaced in 1905 by an immense new hotel, with 400 guest rooms, a main lobby 250 feet long, and a domed dining room that could seat 600. A short walk took guests to the viewing spot.

Within a century of its discovery, the rock profile had become a major tourist attraction and a major part of the area economy. Images of the face appeared on souvenirs, jugs, drinking glasses, elegant china pitchers, boxes, and containers that vied for the attention of travelers who wanted a remembrance of the marvel they had seen.

It was Col. Charles Greenleaf, the owner of the Profile House (and much of the land in the Notch) who first called attention to the fact that the Old Man was in peril. Around 1872 a Boston newspaper mentioned that the profile was in danger of falling, so Greenleaf climbed the mountain. He found that the gigantic boulder that formed the forehead of the face was cracked and the brow was gradually slipping forward. The Appalachian Mountain Club confirmed this observation, and Greenleaf returned with a stone mason and a blacksmith to see if anything could be done to stop the profile's slip into oblivion. It was impossible, they concluded.

But others would not accept that conclusion. The Rev. Guy Roberts of Whitefield loved the profile and, beginning in 1906, he mounted a personal campaign to save it. In 1915 he talked E. H. Geddes, the manager of a Quincy, Massachusetts, stone quarry, into climbing the mountain to determine if anything could be done. Geddes decided that a series of cables and turnbuckles would allow the forehead rock to move with the expansion of ice in the winter but bring the twenty-five-ton rock back into place when the ice melted in the spring. He made a model of his plan and sent it north to Roberts in 1916. Greenleaf immediately accepted the plan and urged the governor and the state to act to save the state's symbol.

On September 25, 1916, in spite of the threat of freezing temperatures and extremely dangerous working conditions, the fifty-three-year-old Geddes started his work. Balanced precariously more than a thousand feet above the valley floor, he laboriously hand drilled holes into the forehead rock. Only four inches of forward movement would send it, and him, crashing down. For eight long days he worked in the cold and ice, attaching devices into the stone and tying the stone to the mountain with heavy iron rods and turnbuckles. Finally, Greenleaf, Roberts, and Geddes had done something to preserve this wonder for posterity.

But, as Roberts and Geddes had foreseen, nature continued its work on the profile. In 1937 Geddes made his last inspection of the face and warned that care should be taken to prevent further movement of the rocks. By 1954 it was discovered that the boulder had moved another three-quarters of an inch toward collapse, and in 1958 another effort was made to preserve the Old Man.

More than fifty tons of metal and other equipment were hauled to the top of the profile for the repairs. New cables and turnbuckles were installed, and an impermeable cap was placed over the wide crack that separated the forehead boulder from the mountain to prevent ice from continuing to push it over the edge.

In 1947 a young man named Niels Neilsen took his fiancee Louise Colburn into the mountains to see the Old Man. Thirteen years later, as a newly hired bridge construction foreman for the New Hampshire Highway Department, he made his first climb to the top of the Old Man's forehead. Eventually, his sons, Bob, Tom, Mike, and David also joined the repair crew, David when he was only eleven years old. Annually, for almost forty years Neils Neilsen and his sons joined in the annual treks to ensure the future of the profile. When Neils was no longer able to lead the way, David took over as the protector of the Old Man.

The crew noticed that dirt and dust were being driven into the cracks and that rain or snow stayed in this paste. When the paste froze, it became a jack, forcing the cracks ever wider. Also, unbelievably, even hikers damaged the profile by breaking through its protective cover by carving their initials in it.

It was a constant battle of measuring slippage, sealing cracks, and repairing the covering that prevented water infiltration. The work required men to suspend themselves out over the edges of the cliff where they swayed in the high winds that buffet the mountaintop. For four decades they succeeded in holding the Great Stone Face together, and almost a million people a year stopped along the highway below to gaze up at the natural wonder.

Then, at some point between May 1 and the morning of May 3, 2003, the unthinkable happened. For two days clouds and rain covered the top of Cannon Mountain so thickly that the profile was hidden from view. It was still early spring in the mountains and snow and ice that had fallen during the winter was melting and refreezing as nighttime temperatures plummeted. Park rangers of Franconia State Park, while on their early morning rounds May 3, glanced up at the profile and rubbed their eyes before looking again. The state's beloved Old Man was gone. No one had seen or heard his fall and even the huge boulders that had formed him could not be found. He had slipped from his high mountain perch and disappeared forever, leaving a void in New Hampshire's soul that many say will never be filled.

A Potpourri of New Hampshire Facts

• New Hampshire has a total area of 9,304 square miles and ranks forty-fourth among the states in size.

• As of the census of 2000, the population of New Hampshire was 1,235,786: 18.9 percent of New Hampshire's population is between the ages of five and seventeen; 30.9 percent are between the ages of twenty-five and forty-four.

• New Hampshire became the ninth state on June 21, 1788.

• There are ten counties in New Hampshire.

• The highest point in the state of New Hampshire is Mount Washington, at 6288 feet in Sargents Purchase, Coos County. The lowest point in New Hampshire is at sea level on the Atlantic coast.

• New Hampshire's nickname is "The Granite State," named for the rock that underlies it and symbolic of the sturdiness of its people. It has a second nickname, The Primary State, for its first-in-the-nation presidential preference primary.

• The state capital is Concord, 1808. The royal capital was at Portsmouth; the colonial capital, at Exeter.

- Manchester is the state's largest city, with a population of 107,000 (2000 census).

- The state bird is the purple finch.

- The state flower is the purple lilac.

- The white birch is the state tree.

- The ladybug is the state insect.

- The state song is "Old New Hampshire," lyrics by John F. Holmes, music by Maurice Hoffman.

- New Hampshire's state motto is "Live Free or Die," first uttered by New Hampshire Revolutionary War hero Gen. John Stark, as a commemoration of the Battle of Bennington, Vermont, where he led the colonists to victory.

- Dartmouth College, at Hanover, was formed in 1769. It is the ninth-oldest college in the United States.

- The original "Uncle Sam," Samuel Wilson, lived in Mason, New Hampshire, his mother's hometown, during the 1780s.

- The Provincial Congress drafted New Hampshire's first constitution on December 21, 1775; it took effect January 5, 1776.

- New Hampshire's second, and present, constitution was ratified on October 31, 1783, and became effective on June 2, 1784. It is the second oldest state constitution and predates the U.S. Constitution by three years.

• Article 10 of the New Hampshire Constitution includes the right of revolution, the only state constitution to do so.

• The New Hampshire State House at Concord was dedicated on June 2, 1819. It is made of 1,650 tons of granite, quarried and dressed locally by state prisoners.

• In 1822 the first free public library in the United States was opened at Dublin.

• Concord lawyer and general Franklin Pierce was elected fourteenth president of the United States in 1852. During his term the "Black Fleet" of the United States forced Japan to open its doors to outside trade, which led to the modernization of Japan.

• Thirty-nine thousand men from New Hampshire served during the Civil War, with casualties of more than 4,000 deaths. The Fifth New Hampshire Volunteers, with a force of 2,600, lost more than 1,500.

• The famed novelist and poet Nathaniel Hawthorne died unexpectedly at Plymouth, New Hampshire. A close friend of President Pierce, he wrote Pierce's biography shortly before he died.

• During 1884 the parents of Robert Frost moved the family to New Hampshire when he was age ten. He later lived at Salem, Derry, Plymouth, and Franconia, writing about half of his poetry in the state.

• Writer and poet John Greenleaf Whittier spent his summers in New Hampshire and wrote often of its folklore and history. He died at the seacoast mansion "Elmhurst" on September 7, 1892.

• The keel of the U.S. Navy's first modern operational submarine was laid at the Portsmouth Navy Yard in 1914. It was launched in 1918. The yard has since built dozens of submarines and continues today as a major repair facility.

• In May 1918, in support of the war effort, the Amoskeag Manufacturing Company of Manchester created the largest United States flag. It was 100 feet by 52 feet and weighed about 500 pounds. It was displayed on company buildings.

• On January 8, 1934, the U.S. Supreme Court issued an order establishing the boundary between New Hampshire and Vermont as the low-water mark on the west bank of the Connecticut River, giving the whole river, except in flood, to New Hampshire.

• In July 1944 the International Monetary Conference was held at Bretton Woods in the Mount Washington Hotel. The conference created the World Bank and the International Monetary Fund and established the U.S. dollar as the standard for international commerce.

• In March 1976 the unknown former governor of Georgia, Jimmy Carter, won the New Hampshire primary. He opened his official campaign for the presidency in New Hampshire, following his nomination by the Democratic Party.

• On July 19, 1985, Christa McAuliffe, a teacher at Concord High School, was chosen to participate in a space shuttle mission from among more than 11,000 applicants. While her students in Concord watched on live television, the shuttle *Challenger* exploded on takeoff on January 28, 1986, killing her and all members of the crew.

Further Reading

Adams, Rachel. *On The Other Hand*. New York: Harper & Row, 1963.

Allen, Everett S. *A Wind to Shake the World: The Story of the 1938 Hurricane*. Boston: Little, Brown, 1976.

Allen, John B. *From Skisport to Skiing: One Hundred Years of an American Sport, 1840–1940*. Amherst: University of Massachusetts Press, 1973.

Brown, Dona. *Inventing New England: Regional Tourism in the Nineteenth Century*. Washington, D.C.: Smithsonian Institution Press, 1995.

Doan, Daniel. *Indian Stream Republic: Settling a New England Frontier*. Hanover, N.H.: University Press of New England, 1997.

Early, Eleanor. *Behold the White Mountains*. Boston: Little, Brown, and Company, 1935.

Hancock, Frances Ann Johnson. *Saving the Great Stone Face*. Franconia, N.H.: Phoenix Publishing/Franconia Area Heritage Council, 1980.

Hareven, Tamara, and Rudolph Langenbach. *Amoskeag: Life and Work in an American Factory City*. New York: Pantheon Press, New York, 1978.

Howe, Nicholas. *Not Without Peril: 150 Years of Misadventure on the Presidential Range of New Hampshire*. Boston: AMC Club Books, 2000.

Kidder, Glen M. *Railway to the Moon*. Littleton, N.H.: Courier Printing Co., 1969.

Kilbourne, Frederick W. *Chronicles of the White Mountains*. Cambridge, Mass.: Houghton Mifflin Company, 1916.

Koop, Allen V. *Stark Decency: German Prisoners of War in a New England Village*. Hanover, N.H.: University Press of New England, 1988.

Maas, Peter. *The Terrible Hours*. New York: HarperCollins, 1999.

McLaughlin, Robert E. *On Church Hill*. Portsmouth, N.H.: St. John's Church, 1982.

Pike, Robert E. *Spiked Boots*. Dublin, N.H.: Yankee Books, 1988.

Pike, Robert E. *Tall Trees Tough Men*. New York: W.W. Norton & Company, 1967.

Proper, David R. *A "Keene" Sense of History*. Porstmouth, N.H.: Peter Randall Publishers, 2002.

Ramsey, Floyd W. *Shrouded Memories*. Littleton, N.H.: Bondcliff Books, 1994.

Randall, Peter E. *Mount Washington, A Guide & Short History*. 3rd ed. Woodstock, Vt.: Countryman Press, 1992.

Stabler, Lois K. (ed.). *Very Poor and of a Lo Make: The Journal of Abner Sanger*. Portsmouth, N.H.: Peter Randall Publishers, 1987.

The New Hampshire Historical Society in Concord, N.H., publishes and sells numerous books on the History of New Hampshire. The Web site www.nhhistory.org has their library catalog and list of publications for sale.

Index